NATIONAL NORTHERN BORDER COUNTERNARCOTICS STRATEGY

Office of National Drug Control Policy

JANUARY 2012

Table of Contents

Introduction

The United States and Canada are not simply allies, not simply neighbors; we are woven together like perhaps no other two countries in the world… [Prime Minister Stephen Harper and I] agreed to a new vision for managing our shared responsibilities—not just at the border but "beyond the border." That means working more closely to improve border security with better screening, new technologies and information-sharing among law enforcement, as well as identifying threats early.

–President Barack Obama, February 4, 2011

Transnational Criminal Organizations (TCOs) operating on both sides of the United States and Canada border are exploiting the international boundary to move proceeds from illegal drugs sold in the United States and Canada and to transport drugs such as marijuana, Ecstasy, meth, and cocaine between the two countries. The border is the longest border between two countries in the world, spanning 5, 225 miles. The United States and Canada recognize that the threat from TCOs is a threat to regional security and stability of both countries. To increase each country's individual security and economic vitality, the United States and Canada must appropriately plan, train, and act together to address threats at the earliest point possible and work toward optimizing joint border management goals. On February 4, 2011, President Barack Obama and Prime Minister Stephen Harper articulated this understanding of shared responsibility for our security in *Beyond the Border: A Joint Vision for Perimeter Security and Economic Competitiveness* (BTB) which, among other things, confirms that the United States and Canada are "staunch allies, vital economic partners, and steadfast friends."

BTB identifies four key areas of cooperation through which Canada and the United States can "pursue a perimeter approach to security, working together within, at, and away from the borders of our two countries." The key areas of cooperation are: Addressing Threats Early; Trade Facilitation, Economic Growth, and Jobs; Integrated Cross-border Law Enforcement; and Critical Infrastructure and Cybersecurity. Through integrated cross-border law enforcement, the United States and Canada will build upon existing relationships, programs, and policies; seek further opportunities to pursue national security by disrupting transnational criminal organizations; and improve our information sharing, allowing us to use our resources more efficiently and effectively to curb the flow of illegal narcotics and money across the Northern border.

This document, the *2012 National Northern Border Counternarcotics Strategy* (*Strategy*), articulates the U.S. framework for the ongoing efforts to reduce the threats on both sides of the border and is guided by the following strategic goal and five strategic objectives:

Strategic Goal

Substantially reduce the flow of illicit drugs and drug proceeds along the Northern border[1].

Strategic Objectives

1. Enhance intelligence and information-sharing capabilities and processes associated with the Northern border;

2. Interdict illicit drugs and illicit drug proceeds at and between the ports of entry along the Northern border;

3. Interdict illicit drugs and illicit drug proceeds in the air and maritime domains along the Northern border;

4. Enhance counterdrug efforts and cooperation with tribal governments along the Northern border; and

5. Disrupt and dismantle transnational criminal organizations operating along the Northern border.

Each of the *Strategy's* five chapters addresses one of the Strategic Objectives by providing specific details and a summary of supporting actions and Federal agencies identified for action. Agencies responsible for leading interagency coordination within each supporting action are underlined in each chapter. To ensure effective implementation of the *Strategy,* Appendix One provides indicators to develop baselines and enable status tracking of the *Strategy's* implementation. Further, Appendix Two includes resources required to enable the relevant National Drug Control Program agencies to successfully implement the *Strategy.* The appendix includes program descriptions and resource information at the FY 2011 enacted level for all efforts included in the *Strategy.*

Because state, local, and tribal law enforcement agencies are key players in border security efforts, enhanced Federal collaboration with these entities is one of the major areas of emphasis in this *Strategy.* This *Strategy,* by building upon existing architecture; identifying needed resources; and enlisting state, local, and tribal law enforcement in a genuine partnership, will enable the Nation to address the threat in a comprehensive manner.

This *Strategy* is submitted pursuant to Public Law 111-356. Public Law 111-356, the Northern Border Counternarcotics Strategy Act of 2010 (Act), requires that not later than 180 days after the date of enactment, and every two years thereafter, the Director of the Office of National Drug Control Policy (ONDCP) shall submit to Congress a Northern Border Counternarcotics Strategy, and that document shall:

1. set forth the strategy of the Federal Government for preventing the illegal trafficking of drugs and drug proceeds across the international border between the United States and Canada, including through and between border ports of entry;

---

1. For the purpose of this document, the phrase "Northern border" refers to the U.S.–Canada border between Maine and Washington State.

2. state the specific roles and responsibilities of each relevant National Drug Control Program agency for implementing the *Strategy*;

3. identify the specific resources required to enable the relevant National Drug Control Program agencies to implement the *Strategy*; and

4. reflect the unique nature of small communities along the international border between the United States and Canada, ongoing cooperation and coordination with Canadian law enforcement authorities, and variations in the volumes of vehicles and pedestrians crossing through ports of entry along the international border between the United States and Canada.

The Act additionally mandates that the *Strategy* incorporate specific content related to cross-border Indian reservations, including (1) a strategy to end the illegal trafficking of drugs to or through Indian reservations on or near the international border between the United States and Canada; and (2) recommendations for additional assistance, if any, needed by tribal law enforcement agencies relating to the *Strategy*, including an evaluation of Federal technical and financial assistance, infrastructure capacity building, and interoperability deficiencies.

This *Strategy* provides an overview of current efforts and broad supporting actions aimed at substantially reducing the flow of illicit drugs and illicit drug proceeds along the Northern border.

Demand Reduction

In addition to the enforcement-focused actions in this *Strategy*, the Administration recognizes the important role prevention plays in reducing the demand for drugs and creating healthier communities. Evidence suggests that the most effective prevention strategies actively engage the communities they serve. Communities can be mobilized to identify, plan, direct resources, and undertake effective action for health promotion and health-enhancing social change. Various Federal, state, local, and tribal programs are underway to build stronger communities.

The United States–Canada Border Drug Threat

Overview

Marijuana and Ecstasy remain the most significant Canadian drug threats to the United States, while the United States remains the primary transit country for cocaine into Canada from South America. While still responsible for significant social harm and public health and safety consequences at the individual and community levels, methamphetamine (meth) and heroin pose much lesser threats to each country, as evidenced by case reporting and limited northbound and southbound seizures.

Illicit drug production in Canada consists mostly of Ecstasy and high potency marijuana, as well as meth. These drugs are produced for consumption in Canada as well as for distribution into illicit U.S. markets. In fact, Canada is the primary source of Ecstasy for North America.

Various groups are involved in the cultivation, production, and distribution of Ecstasy and high potency marijuana in Canada and across our shared border. These groups are generally ethnically aligned, and include Vietnamese-Canadian, Indo-Canadian, Irish-Canadian, and Italian-Canadian organized crime groups; the Hells Angels Motorcycle Club, and independent transnational criminal organizations (TCOs). They are concentrated mainly in the Western Canadian province of British Columbia, as well as the eastern provinces of Ontario and Quebec. Ecstasy and marijuana are smuggled across the border at and between ports of entry (POEs).

The vast, rugged terrain and bodies of water that comprise the U.S.–Canada border pose challenges to law enforcement on both sides, and present vulnerabilities Canada-based TCOs continue to exploit as long as there is limited protection.

> **Drug Demand**
>
> An estimated 22.6 million Americans (8.9 percent) aged 12 or older were current (past month) users of illicit drugs in 2010. The rate of use was similar to the rate in 2009 (8.7 percent). In 2009, the prevalence of use of at least one of six drugs (including cannabis, cocaine or crack, speed, Ecstasy, hallucinogens (excluding salvia) or heroin) in the past-year was approximately 2.8 million Canadians (11.0 percent) aged 15 or older. This represents a decline from the rate of use reported in 2004, at 14.5 percent.
>
> *Sources: 2010 National Survey on Drug Use and Health, September 2011*
>
> *2009 Canadian Alcohol and Drug Use Monitoring Survey.*

An equal and very significant threat along with the movement of illicit drugs across the U.S.–Canada border, is the bi-directional movement of illicit drug proceeds. Illicit proceeds from drug sales in the U.S. and Canada provide TCOs the economic resources to continue or further expand drug production, distribution, and sales. Bulk cash smuggling and money service businesses (MSBs) facilitate money laundering in both directions along the Northern border. Illicit proceeds from the sale of marijuana and Ecstasy in the U.S., and cocaine in Canada are often smuggled across the Northern border. Canadian law enforcement has also identified cases where U.S. drug traffickers travel to Canada to place illicit proceeds in Canadian MSBs and banks.

Current Situation

Ecstasy and Synthetics

Historically, MDMA (3, 4-methylenedioxymethamphetamine), is the hallucinogenic substance commonly found in the drug sold as "Ecstasy." Ecstasy tablets are no longer just MDMA, but rather a cocktail of chemicals. Samples of Ecstasy analyzed by Drug Enforcement Administration (DEA) laboratories contain meth, ketamine, caffeine, dimethylsulfone, N-benzylpiperazine (BZP), and trifluoromethylpiperazine (TFMPP), in addition to MDMA.

Ecstasy production occurs primarily in British Columbia, and to a lesser extent in Ontario and Quebec. The Royal Canadian Mounted Police (RCMP) reported in 2009 that 12 clandestine Ecstasy laboratories were seized throughout Canada; half of the laboratories seized in British Columbia were of significant size and able to produce multi-thousand tablet quantities.[2]

Case reporting and intelligence indicate that ethnic Chinese groups are primarily responsible for the production of Ecstasy in Canada. These groups procure the necessary precursor chemicals from China, including MDP2P,[3] the primary chemical needed to produce Ecstasy. In May 2008, the Canada Border Services Agency (CBSA) seized 3.7 tons of MDP2P, smuggled from China into the Port of Vancouver.

Ecstasy at a Glance

- Retail prices per tablet are CAD$10 - $20 in Canada while it is USD$5 - $70 in the United States, depending on the region of the country.

- The price per pill in Los Angeles ranges from $3-$11, while the price per pill in New York City ranges from $3 - $25.

- The market in the United States is small compared to marijuana, but it is steady and lucrative.

- It is no longer exclusively viewed as a "rave" or club drug, resulting in expanded distribution to nontraditional abusers.

- The 2010 National Survey on Drug Use and Health (NSDUH) reported that 695,000 individuals, aged 12 and older, used Ecstasy in the last month, a decrease from 760,000 individuals the previous year.

In September 2010, the Department of Justice (DOJ) reported that a member of a Canada-based Asian TCO was sentenced in the United States to 10 years in prison for his role in drug trafficking from Canada to the United States. The TCO was responsible for smuggling more than 10,000 kilograms of marijuana and 300,000 Ecstasy tablets into the United States over a two-year period. The drugs were obtained from various Asian organized crime groups in Canada. According to DOJ, the group negotiated the prices and terms of delivery with the drug producers in Canada, and smuggled approximately $25 million dollars out of the United States.

Ethnic Vietnamese, Indian, Eastern European, outlaw motorcycle and independent/loosely structured groups are also involved in Ecstasy manufacturing and trafficking to the United States.

Ready availability of Ecstasy has enabled distributors to expand their customer base of young adult Caucasians to include new user groups, most notably African American and Hispanic users. Asian TCOs have begun distributing Ecstasy to African-American and Hispanic street gangs, which distribute

---

2. RCMP National Clandestine Laboratory Activity Report, 2009
3. MDP2P (3, 4 methylenedioxyphenyl-2-Propanone)

this and other illicit drugs in markets throughout the United States, most notably in the Southeast, Southwest, and Great Lakes Regions.

Canada-based TCOs responsible for the production of synthetic drugs continue to demonstrate a willingness to utilize whichever chemicals are readily available to them, as evidenced in the increased appearance of Ecstasy-like substances in recent years. For example, in 2009, law enforcement found a significant increase in seizures of BZP/TFMPP tablets. Of particular concern were the new presence and seizure of BZP/TFMPP tablets in and around schools in the United States and the mimic drug's resemblance to candy or children's vitamins. The risk of accidental ingestion by young children is of significant Federal, state, and local concern.[4] Significant quantities of BZP/TFMPP tablets were traced back to Canadian sources.

While Canadian-produced meth currently poses a limited threat to the United States, clandestine production in Canada remained steady between 2008 and 2009, and sporadic southbound seizures have occurred and continue to occur. In March 2011, U.S. law enforcement authorities seized 20 kilograms of meth powder and two kilograms of ketamine powder and made one arrest; the drugs were smuggled from an area of the Saint Regis Mohawk Reservation in Quebec to upstate New York, and were intended for further distribution to cities in the eastern United States. The size, location, and substances encountered make this a significant seizure.

Increased supplies of gamma-hydroxybutyrate (GHB) and ketamine circulating in the Canadian illicit market since 2009 suggest renewed interest in these recreational drugs for their use as alternative or supplemental substances to Ecstasy or meth. GHB and ketamine, closely associated with the rave and youth-oriented drug culture, are an increasing concern for Canadian authorities. The availability of GHB is more widespread throughout Canada, facilitated by the simple process required to produce the drug. Ketamine is procured either through diversion of pharmaceutical supply or by importation, mostly from Southeast Asia. Ketamine and GHB enter the U.S. markets via domestic production, Internet procurement, or diversion from legitimate sources. However, the above-mentioned ketamine seizure in New York illustrates the potential for cross-border trafficking of other synthetic substances.

Marijuana

Marijuana is the most widely abused illicit drug in the United States and Canada. While most marijuana in both the United States and Canada is cultivated to supply domestic demand, distribution of high potency marijuana from Canada into the United States remains a concern.

In Canada, high potency marijuana plants are typically cultivated indoors; significant cultivation has been identified primarily in British Columbia, as well as in Ontario and Quebec. Groups and individuals involved in the production of this high potency marijuana, often referred to as "BC Bud," have established sophisticated indoor marijuana growing operations ("grows"), typically in residential homes. Traffickers significantly modify the houses to accommodate elaborate lighting, irrigation, and ventilation systems. These agronomic techniques, coupled with plant selection, contribute to production of high potency plants.

---

4. DEA Drug Intelligence Brief, DEA-NCT-DIB-035-10, February 2010

Case reporting indicates Asian criminal groups, particularly those of Vietnamese descent, are the primary operators of grows in western Canada (British Columbia) and the western United States (California, Washington). Ethnic Indian and Caucasian growers and criminal groups with ties to the Hells Angels Motorcycle Club are also identified as grow operators and/or involved in the distribution of Canadian-produced marijuana. Canadian-based Irish and Italian organized crime and those with ties to Hells Angels Motorcycle Club are involved in marijuana production and smuggling in eastern Canada (Ontario, Quebec) and the eastern United States (upstate New York and northern New England).

In addition, Vietnamese TCOs, in some cases with ties to Canada, have expanded their production operations into the United States. The TCOs have moved their indoor marijuana grow activities to the United States in an effort to decrease transportation costs and limit the risk of seizure associated with smuggling marijuana across the Northern border.

In the past three years, the U.S. Attorney's Office for the Northern District of New York has indicted over 100 individuals in a series of investigations which demonstrate the St. Regis Reservation is being used by a number of large-scale trafficking organizations to facilitate smuggling activities. These organizations smuggled marijuana to the Northeast, Mid-Atlantic, and Midwest regions. Among the arrested/indicted, there were four Regional Priority Organization Targets (RPOTs). For example, in July 2009, the U.S. Attorney's Office for the Northern District of New York indicted three members of a large-scale, Canadian-based organization on drug trafficking charges. The TCO smuggled marijuana across the Northern border for distribution to members in New Hampshire, New York, and Pennsylvania and smuggled currency back to Canada.[5] The organization smuggled the marijuana in heat-sealed bags inside large duffel bags from Canada through the Saint Regis Mohawk Indian Reservation and a secluded wooded area near Churubusco, New York.[6]

Cocaine

The vast majority of cocaine that crosses the U.S.–Canada border is northbound into Canada. Cocaine destined for Canada originates in South America and transits a variety of countries in South and Central America and the Caribbean. Shipments can transit one or more countries prior to entering Canada. The United States has long been the predominant transit point for cocaine smuggled into Canada, although a shift in smuggling patterns in 2010 suggests the preeminent role of the United

Cocaine – Ecstasy - Marijuana

A nexus exists between marijuana and Ecstasy smuggling from Canada, and cocaine transiting the United States into Canada. Canada-based TCOs, particularly Asian groups in British Columbia and Caucasian and Outlaw Motorcycle Gangs from Quebec and Ontario, utilize their trafficking networks, which are based on social and familial ties, to smuggle Ecstasy and high potency marijuana across the border. Connections are then made with cocaine distributors in the United States, and an agreed-upon quantity of cocaine is exchanged for Ecstasy and/or marijuana. The Ecstasy and/or marijuana are then further distributed to other regions of the United States. Bulk currency associated with these illicit drug transactions, particularly in upstate New York, is smuggled to southern California, where it is used to purchase cocaine, which is then smuggled to Canada for distribution. The cocaine sells for approximately $25,000 - $28,000 USD per kilogram in the United States, and approximately $38,000 – $43,000 per kilogram in Canada.

---

5. U.S. Department of Justice (DOJ), Drug Enforcement Administration (DEA), Press Release, "International Drug Ring Charged," July 7, 2009.
6. U.S. DOJ, DEA, Press Release, "International Drug Ring Charged," July 7, 2009.

States as a transshipment point may be diminishing, as traffickers ship cocaine directly to Canada via air and maritime conveyances.

Occasionally, cocaine is further smuggled from Canada to Australia. While the greatest cocaine threat to Australia is from Mexican and South American TCOs, investigative reporting indicates instances where sources of supply have ties to Canada. Kilogram quantities of cocaine sell for between $156,000–$200,000 USD in Australia, presenting a tempting option for drug traffickers.

Major Trafficking Corridors, Groups, and Methods

Canadian-based TCOs, including ethnic Vietnamese criminal groups, Indo-Canadian individuals, members and associates of the Hells Angels Motorcycle Club, and other criminal groups are involved in cross-border Ecstasy and marijuana smuggling between Canada and the U.S. These groups may arrange to pay for cocaine, which is typically supplied by Mexican TCOs in the United States, with proceeds from the sale of the marijuana and/or Ecstasy. They may even exchange or barter for cocaine with their U.S.-based intermediaries. Some Canadian TCOs have direct contact with Mexican and/or other sources of cocaine supply in Latin America. In some cases, the cocaine by-passes the U.S. entirely, or shipments may transit U.S. territory en route to Canada.

Illegal drugs are smuggled across our shared border via a number of modes. Ecstasy, marijuana and cocaine are smuggled via personal vehicles, commercial trucks, buses, planes (small personal planes/helicopters and couriers on commercial airlines), trains, vessels, all-terrain vehicles, and snowmobiles. TCOs recruit individuals to carry drugs on their person at and between POEs in all domains. For example, in March 2011, a female U.S. citizen traveling by bus from Canada via Buffalo, New York was in possession of 34,000 Ecstasy tablets; the tablets were strapped to her body to appear as if she were pregnant. The woman was subsequently arrested.

Canadian-based TCOs smuggle Ecstasy and marijuana through and between POEs along the entire U.S.–Canada border. However, the primary smuggling corridors used by drug traffickers are areas in the vicinity of Blaine, Washington; Detroit, Michigan; and Buffalo, New York. Canadian-based TCOs in Ontario and Quebec utilize the Saint Regis Mohawk Reservation and some members of its community to smuggle Ecstasy and marijuana into the United States. This region is inviting to smugglers for a number of reasons. The Reservation straddles the U.S.–Canada border allowing tribal members to pass freely over the international border. The tribe's territory also includes a portion of the St. Lawrence River, with the U.S.–Canada border running through the river. Law enforcement on either side of the U.S.–Canada border have jurisdiction solely on their respective sides, although the May 2009 agreement for Integrated Cross-Border Maritime Law Enforcement Operations (ShipRider) which formalizes integrated joint law enforcement teams along the maritime border will reduce the ability of criminal organizations to take advantage of jurisdictional limits.

Weapons Smuggling

Weapons smuggling on the Northern border is not at the levels seen along the United States Southwest border. In 2010, 1800 weapons recovered in crimes were traced back to United States dealers, not legally registered to Canadian citizens. Of those, all but 99 were recovered at the border.

While minimal in comparison to the Southwest border, there have been instances of weapons obtained by straw purchase or TCOs exchanging drugs for weapons in the United States and smuggling them into Canada.

Further west, Native American reservations in northern Washington State are utilized as smuggling routes. Mexican drug traffickers are known to be using northern Washington reservations and tribal members to further their illicit activities. The Nooksack Tribe in northern Washington and Skway First Nation in British Columbia are sister reservations that share ancestral ties and familial members. As a result, frequent uncontrolled cross-border travel of tribal members occurs; opportunities traffickers exploit.

DEA and U.S. Immigration and Customs Enforcement (ICE) investigations in the Pacific Northwest show numerous drug smuggling groups using maritime routes in the Puget Sound, the Strait of Georgia, and the Strait of Juan de Fuca. Large-scale maritime drug seizures have occurred over the past ten years at numerous locations in the waters between Vancouver, British Columbia and Washington State. In March 2010, a total of 1,001 kilograms of cocaine was seized from a sailboat that was en-route to Vancouver from South America, resulting in the arrest of a Canadian citizen and a Mexican national. In May 2010, 547 pounds of marijuana were seized from suspects who were operating a rigid-hull inflatable boat coming from British Columbia to the north coast of the Olympic Peninsula near Port Angeles, Washington. In December 2010, two jet skis were found abandoned at Lummi Island, very near Lummi Tribal land (near Bellingham, Washington) following a seizure of 203 kilograms of cocaine in Bellingham from a known cross-border TCO. The jet skis were directly linked to the same cross-border TCO, whose members own and operate several different water vessels in that area.

Outlook

While the threats to North America along the U.S.–Canada border are continually shifting, it is not anticipated that a significant change in trafficker activities will occur in the near term. However, there remains potential for new developments. Instances of Ecstasy seizures will remain relatively stable, based on the continued availability of the drug and the niche market Ecstasy maintains. Southbound seizures of marijuana may decrease as a result of Asian TCOs establishing indoor marijuana growing operations throughout the United States. Cocaine will continue to transit the United States en route to Canada, and traffickers will continue to seek new routes and means of transportation for this and other drugs. Tribal lands have been a conduit for illicit activity for a number of years. This activity will continue because of reservation geography, the ability of tribal members to move freely between countries, and the willingness of drug traffickers to exploit these opportunities. Further, TCOs globally are expanding their operations while also diversifying their activities, potentially resulting in gaining the logistical support for acts of terrorism or the development of human smuggling networks.[7] Understanding these trends, the supporting actions outlined in the *Strategy* will ultimately reduce the flow of illicit drugs and drug proceeds, and reduce the potential for other harmful activity committed by TCOs, along the Northern border.

---

7. "2011 Strategy to Combat Transnational Organized Crime." July 2011.

Cooperation with Canada

Background

Historically, Canada has been a vital treaty partner, under both the U.S.–Canada Extradition Treaty and the Mutual Legal Assistance Treaty (MLAT) on Criminal Matters. Leaders from the United States and Canada meet frequently and maintain close and cordial relations, which are invaluable in addressing and resolving sensitive bilateral law enforcement issues.

The U.S. law enforcement community's relationship with Canada is essential and effective. Both countries value this relationship and recognize its key role in assuring the respective security and safety of their citizens. U.S. law enforcement officers at all levels cooperate with Canadian counterparts daily, and increasingly, U.S. and Canadian prosecutors pursue collaborative investigations. Most Federal law enforcement agencies are represented at the U.S. Embassy in Ottawa and in greater collective numbers than in any other U.S. Embassy. The United States values its relationship with Canada and respects its sovereignty, as well as the privacy and civil rights of its citizens.

U.S. and Canadian Federal agencies cooperate with state, local, and tribal partners to interact effectively from the field up through legal and policy management to ensure our two countries meet our shared objectives in combating the production, trafficking, and distribution of illegal drugs, while allowing for the legitimate cross-border flow of people, goods, and services. The DEA, ICE, Bureau of Alcohol, Tobacco, Firearms and Explosives (ATF), and U.S. Customs and Border Protection (CBP) have Country Attaché (or Assistant Attaché) Offices in Ottawa and Vancouver. ICE additionally has offices in Toronto and Montreal. The Federal Bureau of Investigation (FBI) has a Legal Attaché Office in Ottawa and sub-offices in Vancouver and Toronto.

For such cross-border drug issues, DHS components partner with Canadian law enforcement agencies to investigate international smuggling crimes. These investigations are coordinated with the DEA, which is the single point of contact for U.S. drug related matters in the foreign environment and for ensuring that investigations comply with relevant U.S. and Canadian government protocols.[8] The United States and Canada also exchange forfeited assets through a bilateral asset-sharing agreement and share information to prevent, investigate, and prosecute any offense against U.S. or Canadian customs laws through a Customs Mutual Assistance Agreement.

The following initiatives represent the spectrum of existing bi-lateral law enforcement collaboration.

Cross Border Crime Forum

The United States and Canada work closely to stop the production, trafficking, and distribution of illegal narcotics. The United States focuses its bilateral cooperation with Canada through the Cross-Border Crime Forum (CBCF), established in 1997 to facilitate cooperation among law enforcement bodies to promote effective investigations of cross-border crime. Under the leadership of the Attorney General, the Secretary of Homeland Security (DHS), the Minister of Public Safety Canada (PS), and the Minister and Attorney General of the Department of Justice Canada (Justice Canada), the CBCF brings together senior law enforcement officials and prosecutors to address a number of cross-border issues, including

---

8. Per the Reorganization Plan No. 2 of 1973 and DEA-ICE Interagency Agreement (June 2009).

Integrated Cross-Border Maritime Law Enforcement Operations "ShipRider" Pilots

Starting in 2005, the USCG, in coordination with ICE, launched a bi-national operation conducted under agreement between the U.S. and Canada that allows law enforcement personnel from both countries to conduct integrated law enforcement vessel patrols to prevent, detect, and investigate criminal activities in shared waterways. The ICMLEO "ShipRider" operation removes the international maritime boundary as a barrier to law enforcement by enabling seamless, continuous law enforcement operations across the border. ICMLEO ShipRider facilitates cross-border surveillance and interdiction, is a force multiplier and serves as a model for other U.S.-Canadian cross-border law enforcement initiatives. The USCG has worked with ICE, CBP, and the RCMP and its partners to conduct ICMLEO ShipRider pilots; the 2006 Super Bowl XL; 2007 efforts around Cornwall Island in the St. Lawrence River; 2009 Pre-Olympic Exercise, 2010 Vancouver, BC Winter Olympics, Vancouver, BC Paralympics; and the G8 and G20 events in Toronto, ON. The IMCLEO Framework Agreement document was signed by DHS and Director, Public Safety Canada in May 2009. The Canadian Parliament must ratify this agreement. Preparations are underway for development of standard procedures and training in anticipation of ratification. Additional work is underway to develop standard operating procedures while waiting for legislative approval to fully implement this program. The pilot operations are the proof of concept and the catalyst for the development of a well–developed, integrated cross-border maritime operational concept.

narcotics trafficking. Increasingly, the CBCF is viewed around the world as an example of how countries can work together to improve bilateral and cross-border law enforcement cooperation.

During the November 9-10, 2010 CBCF Ministerial, the four co-chairs, the Attorneys General for the United States and Canada, the Minister for Public Safety and the Secretary of DHS presented information and discussed issues such as integrated border law enforcement, incitement to terrorism, undercover operations, and terrorist travel. During the CBCF Ministerial, CBSA, ICE, and CBP signed a Memorandum of Understanding (MOU) to share information related to currency seizures on a case-by-case basis that will assist both countries in fighting money laundering and terrorist financing. This MOU will assist the United States and Canada in sharing information helpful in disrupting and dismantling drug production, trafficking, and distribution networks.

During the CBCF Ministerial, officials underscored the importance of a shared vision for border security and highlighted progress made by the United States and Canada over the past year to safeguard the critical resources, infrastructure, and citizens of both nations, focusing on streamlining information sharing and enforcement efforts and enhancing the ability of both countries to identify and respond to a wide range of threats. They also discussed the report, *Identity-Related Crime: A Threat Assessment*, as well as joint cross-border operations, such as the Integrated Cross-Border Maritime Law Enforcement Operations (ShipRider).

Integrated Cross-border Maritime Law Enforcement Operations (ICMLEO)

On May 26, 2009, the United States and Canada signed the ICMLEO Framework Agreement on ICMLEO ["ShipRider"] designating the USCG and RCMP as the central authorities for ICMLEO. Once Canada passes implementing legislation, the agreement will allow the exchange of cross-designated officers (ShipRiders) on a permanent basis to perform seamless maritime law enforcement operations along and across the

U.S.-Canadian maritime border. ICMLEO ShipRider is a concept of operations that has already become an invaluable operational tool. Used along with intelligence and investigative-driven operations, it will provide a seamless law enforcement process that will be less taxing on personnel and resources while providing more efficient and effective response to criminal activity in shared waterways. The ICMLEO ShipRider program will enable the RCMP, ICE, CBP, USCG, and other law enforcement agencies to cross-train personnel, share resources, and utilize each other's vessels within the territorial waters of both countries. ICMLEO ShipRider will diminish the ability of drug traffickers to use the international border as a way to evade pursuit by either U.S. or Canadian law enforcement officers.

ICMLEO ShipRider preparatory training is conducted in two ten-day courses per year at the USCG's Maritime Law Enforcement Academy located at the Federal Law Enforcement Training Center (FLETC) in Charleston, South Carolina and is attended by USCG, RCMP, and other Federal, state, provincial, local, and tribal law enforcement personnel.

Integrated Border Enforcement Teams (IBETs)

Canada and the United States have cooperated since 1997 through 15 Integrated Border Enforcement Team (IBET) geographical regions along the Northern border, which are now models for cooperation between the U.S. and Canada. IBET operational interdiction teams, composed of CBP, ICE, USCG, RCMP, and CBSA, operate in 24 locations along the Northern border, including four locations where Canadian and American intelligence analysts are co-located. IBETs work in an integrated land, air, and marine environment within their authorities at and along the border and complement the authorities of other U.S. law enforcement agencies. ICMLEO ShipRider is designed to be the maritime operational arm of the IBETs.

Border Enforcement Security Task forces (BESTs)

U.S. and Canada integrated investigations occur in part through the 22 ICE-led BESTs. The three Northern Border

> **Buffalo BEST**
>
> On August 27, 2008, CBP Officers encountered a third party passenger vehicle/van driven by a 20 year old male subject entering the U.S. from Canada at the Lewiston Bridge, Lewiston, NY. The subject stated he was picking up a friend at the Buffalo airport. CBP inspection of the stow-and-go seating compartment under the seats revealed 58 bags of multi colored pills which were determined to contain approximately 292,000 tabs of ecstasy (approx 88 kgs), $82,940 in cash, and a quantity of suspected steroids and needles. The subject cooperated with Buffalo BEST and assisted in furthering the investigation by heading to Atlanta to deliver the contents of the vehicle. A controlled delivery to Atlanta was coordinated with ICE, which resulted in an additional arrest and $74,000 in U.S. currency. As a result of Canadian BEST members on the Buffalo BEST, the source of supply and additional managers of activity were immediately identified in Canada and timely enforcement actions were taken. Sentences ranged for the arrested subjects from 37 months to 97 months imprisonment.

BESTs incorporate personnel from ICE, CBP, USCG, CBSA, RCMP and other key U.S. and Canadian Federal, state, provincial, local, and tribal agencies. BESTs were developed as a comprehensive approach in 2005 to identify, investigate, disrupt, and dismantle transnational criminal organizations (TCOs) that pose significant threats to border security. The BEST is a proven investigative task force that recognizes the unique resources and capabilities of all participating law enforcement partners, and is built upon the proven pillars of *co-location* and *cross-designation*. Recognizing that TCOs have expanded dramatically in size, scope, and influence in the last decade, BEST operates in line with the *Strategy to Combat*

Transnational Organized Crime[9] by integrating U.S. and international law enforcement partners to combat transnational organized crime. This enables each BEST senior field manager to shape a dynamic, flexible response to local circumstances.

Along the Northern border, BESTs are currently located in Blaine, Washington; Detroit, Michigan; and Buffalo, New York. Additionally, ICE plans to stand-up a BEST in Massena, New York by the end of 2011. These BESTs provide extensive investigation capability at and around the POEs in their respective areas. ICE cross-designation as "customs officers" is essential to successful BEST operations. Cross-designated foreign, state, provincial, local, and tribal law enforcement officers enjoy the same authorities and protections afforded to their ICE customs officer counterparts, effectively eliminating the border as an impediment to law enforcement that has historically been exploited by criminal organizations. The BEST program benefits from the co-located participation, resources, and experience drawn from over 55 state, provincial, and local police departments.

> **Drugged Driving Cooperation**
>
> In July 2011, ONDCP, the Government of Canada, Canadian Centre on Substance Abuse, and the European Monitoring Centre for Drugs and Drug Addiction hosted the first International Symposium on Drugs and Driving in Montreal, Canada. Over the course of the symposium, convening practitioners and experts engaged in this global initiative and improved international collaboration in order to strengthen policy, legislation, health and safety, enforcement and prevention efforts on drugs and driving.

This co-location provides invaluable resources and expertise to provide a comprehensive approach to investigating TCOs. Critical to the success of each Northern border BEST is the participation of Canadian law enforcement agencies (including CBSA, RCMP, Ontario Provincial Police, Niagara Regional Police Service, Toronto Police Service, Windsor Police Service, and Amherstburg Police Service).

DEA Task Forces

DEA has numerous existing task forces along the Northern border, from Bangor, ME to Bellingham, WA. These Task Forces focus on international drug trafficking organizations engaging in criminal activity in both the United States and Canada. The Task Forces utilize state and local law enforcement officers to act as a force multiplier for DEA's enforcement efforts, facilitate the coordination and deconfliction process, ensure there is no duplication of effort, and counternarcotics-related activities are within the established protocols. While Canadian law enforcement personnel are not directly assigned to DEA task forces, the Northern border DEA task forces cooperate regularly with the DEA offices in Canada and Canadian counterparts on cross-border counter-narcotics-related activities.

Synthetic Drug Projects

Project MOLE (Monitoring of Laboratory Equipment) is a project under the G-8, with the purpose of developing a framework to prevent the diversion of licit laboratory equipment/apparatus used in the synthesis or production of controlled drugs and substances in the clandestine laboratory environment. Canada is spearheading this effort to gather intelligence on the movement of laboratory equipment, specifically tableting machines. Canada recently led a project to gather information from the G-8 countries on companies that manufacture and trade in tableting machines, with the aim of determining how many companies there are. Europol, through Project Synergy, will gather the information to

---

9. http://www.whitehouse.gov/administration/eop/nsc/transnational-crime

determine the scope of the problem posed by the movement of tableting machines used in Canada to manufacture Ecstasy tablets.

Canada participates in Project Prism, targeting synthetic drug chemicals, and is a member of the North American working group. Canada has agreed to participate in Operation PAAD, an initiative under Project Prism, to monitor the trade in phenyl acetic acid (PAA), which can be made into phenyl-2-propanone (P2P) and further into meth, and its esters and derivatives.

Financial Investigations

The Financial Intelligence Unit (FIU) of the United States, the Department of the Treasury's Financial Crimes Enforcement Network (FinCEN), and the FIU of Canada, Financial Transactions and Reports Analysis Centre (FINTRAC), cooperate in several ways, including the sharing of financial intelligence information to support terrorist financing and money laundering cases, including drug-related money laundering. FinCEN and FINTRAC work closely within the Egmont Group, an international body of anti-money laundering organizations from 127 jurisdictions. Each FIU also regulates a range of financial institutions to increase their vigilance against criminal abuse in addition to requiring recordkeeping and reporting obligations to assist law enforcement with following the money.

Additional Forums

Project North Star is a bi-national, multi-agency forum that further strives to enhance existing communication, cooperation, and partnerships between U.S. and Canadian law enforcement personnel. The aim is to promote and improve cross-border networking, intelligence gathering and sharing, targeting, prosecution, training, and coordinated planning among local, state/provincial, and Federal law enforcement. This cooperation also facilitates the exchange of "best practices" and effective utilization of assets and resources.

The United States Marshals Service (USMS) and the Toronto Police Service co-host the annual International Fugitive Investigators Conference (IFIC). Established in 1999 to address transnational fugitives who cross the shared border, the forum provides a venue for continued cooperation between U.S. and Canadian law enforcement authorities. Each year, partners from local, state/provincial and Federal agencies unite to teach investigative techniques, educate on bi-lateral treaties, encourage intelligence and information sharing, and promote law enforcement best practices.

Judicial Cooperation

The United States and Canada are parties to an extradition treaty that came into force in 1976, and was amended by two Protocols that came into effect in 1991 and 2003. Both Canada and the United States utilize the treaty in making requests for extradition, though the bulk of requests are from the United States. In 2010, about half of the extradition requests received from and sent to Canada involved narcotics offenses. A little more than ten percent of the Canadian requests currently pending in the United States involve narcotics offenses, as well.

Despite the strong law enforcement and judicial relationship between the United States and Canada, extradition from Canada can still be difficult and slow. One reason for this difficulty is that Canadian law requires the United States to set forth a *prima facie* case, higher than the U.S. extradition standard of probable cause, and may require the substantial disclosure of information. Canada's judicial process also allows fugitives to readily seek and obtain bail, even after the same courts have found them extraditable, and to obtain numerous continuances, which prolong the extradition process.

The United States and Canada are also parties to a MLAT that entered into force on January 24, 1990. Almost two-thirds of the requests for assistance are from the United States to Canada. A little less than a quarter of those cases involve narcotics offenses. The United States has to meet a very high standard in order for requests to be executed under Canadian law, including requests for records held by third parties. Canada's privacy laws and views on the application of the Canadian Charter require U.S. officials to make formal MLAT requests to obtain evidence where informal sharing may be more appropriate (e.g., driver's license or passport information).

Chapter 1: Intelligence and Information Sharing

Background

Law enforcement and other agencies participate in strong cooperative efforts to address the expanding range of interrelated challenges along the Northern border, from drug and human smuggling into the United States and Canada, to the transit of arms, bulk cash, and money laundering across the Northern border. These initiatives have led to a substantial improvement in the combined intelligence capabilities of Federal, state, local, tribal, and international partners along the Northern border. Progress in information sharing has paralleled this increase in capabilities, as improved technology and new information-sharing protocols have expanded collection, analysis, and dissemination capabilities between and among partners at all levels.

This chapter addresses specific intelligence programs and activities designed to inform and support decision makers and operators with Northern border counternarcotics responsibilities. U.S. Federal, state, local, and tribal law enforcement agencies with Northern border counternarcotics responsibilities will benefit from enhanced intelligence sharing and information collection, analysis, and dissemination. The need to leverage existing capabilities, such as the El Paso Intelligence Center (EPIC), and programs to strengthen support to Northern border enforcement efforts is also addressed.

Through bilateral cooperation, the United States and Canadian Governments are expanding the nature and scope of their intelligence and enforcement effectiveness. As the operational environment of the Northern border continues to evolve in line with the Administration's expanded border control initiatives, so too will the demand for the comprehensive, relevant, and timely strategic and operational intelligence necessary to sustain effective operations. Long-term planning and resource allocation are guided by strategic intelligence. Individual agencies have developed initiatives to address the range of interrelated challenges on the Northern border. The interagency community must ensure these efforts are coordinated and mutually supportive.

Over the next few years, the focus will be on merging overlapping agency initiatives; improving the delivery of relevant, timely, fully integrated intelligence; and streamlining the information sharing and coordination process among all agencies dedicated to protecting the Northern border from the illicit flow of drugs and associated threats.

> ### El Paso Intelligence Center
>
> The El Paso Intelligence Center (EPIC) has a robust program to provide responses to questions about illicit activity in the United States. EPIC has provided responses to 141 Requests for Information to U.S. Law Enforcement along the Northern border during the past 18 months. Further, the Domestic Highway Enforcement Unit, National License Plate Reader program, Air Investigative Unit, and Research and Analysis Section support Northern border operations.

Supporting Actions

Collection

1. Enhance coordination of intelligence collection among the U.S. Federal, state, local, tribal and Canadian law enforcement agencies with Northern border counternarcotics responsibilities.

Develop a coordinated counternarcotics intelligence requirements process across U.S. Federal, state, local, and tribal counternarcotics agencies. Increasing responsibilities related to counterterrorism and homeland security have placed multiple, competing demands on the intelligence functions of law enforcement agencies and Intelligence Community organizations. Coordination and integration of intelligence requirements processes reduces strain on the entire system, enables increased productivity, eliminates the misdirection of duplicative assets, and creates a "go-to" point for intelligence needs. Sustained efforts will be made to coordinate existing and developing intelligence requirements management processes and, where appropriate, incorporate state, local, and tribal interests in such processes. Opportunities for regular feedback among all counternarcotics enforcement customers will be included in intelligence requirements management processes. **Action: DOJ/DEA, DHS/CBP, DHS/ICE, DHS/I&A, DHS/USCG, DOI, DOJ/FBI, DOJ/NDIC, EPIC, ODNI, ONDCP/HIDTA, USDA/USFS**

Integrate Northern border-related technical and non-technical intelligence collection capabilities carried out by both law enforcement and other organizations. Technical collection capabilities and programs along the Northern border, such as thermal camera systems, License Plate Readers (LPRs), Mobile Surveillance Systems, Unmanned Aircraft Systems (UAS), national distress and command and control networks, and Remote Video Surveillance Systems will be deployed and carefully coordinated among participating agencies. Non-technical law enforcement intelligence collection efforts such as Reports Officers and special field intelligence and debriefing programs will be enhanced and better coordinated. Interagency forums and agreements will also be established to facilitate partnerships and coordination. **Action: DOJ/DEA, DHS/CBP, DHS/ICE, DHS/I&A, DHS/USCG, DOJ, DOJ/OCDETF, EPIC, ODNI, ONDCP/HIDTA**

Analysis

2. Ensure appropriate intelligence activities in support of Northern border counternarcotics efforts, including collaboration with Canadian counterparts.

Ensure the necessary operational intelligence support is available, based on available resources, to frontline organizations to meet operational demands. Partnerships between law enforcement and intelligence entities will be strengthened by identifying opportunities to co-locate and integrate our intelligence activities and offer reciprocal opportunities to our Canadian colleagues, consistent with applicable laws and authorities. Building on existing agreements and joint facilities, agencies will share the opportunities and then coordinate related activities with their respective Country Office Attachés in Canada. **Action: DOJ/DEA, DHS/CBP, DHS/ICE, DHS/I&A, DHS/USCG, DOJ, DOJ/FBI, ODNI, ONDCP/HIDTA**

Develop a coordinated intelligence production planning process across U.S. Federal, state, local, and tribal counternarcotics agencies. Agencies will survey potential consumers to ensure their intelligence products are meeting the needs of border operators. In addition to strategic intelligence analysis to guide executive level decision makers, law enforcement customers on the front lines – in the counternarcotics and homeland security effort – need actionable intelligence to inform and support operational decisions. Efforts to link intelligence to operations will be improved and better coordinated. Greater emphasis will be placed on ensuring intelligence products contain valid operational links or leads and add value to interdiction and investigative activities. Efforts to exploit seizure and investigative information for tactically relevant intelligence will also be enhanced through greater coordination. **Action: <u>DOJ/DEA</u>, DHS/CBP, DHS/ICE, DHS/I&A, DHS/USCG, DOI, DOJ/ATF, DOJ/FBI, DOJ/NDIC, DOJ/OCDETF, EPIC, NSA, ODNI, ONDCP/HIDTA, Treasury, USDA/USFS,**

Collaborate and coordinate on the development of joint intelligence products among U.S. Federal, state, local, tribal and Canadian counterparts. Elements in the intelligence, Federal law enforcement, and state, local, and tribal law enforcement communities regularly produce a variety of assessments related to the Northern border. These products range from comprehensive national assessments to more issue-specific or localized assessments. Agencies will establish mechanisms to coordinate the production of intelligence assessments related to Northern border counternarcotics threats and ensure as wide as possible distribution of those products. **Action: <u>DOJ/DEA</u>, DOD, DHS/CBP, DHS/ICE, DHS/I&A, DHS/ USCG, DOI, DOJ/ATF, DOJ/FBI, DOJ/NDIC, DOJ/OCDETF, EPIC, ODNI, ONDCP/HIDTA, Treasury/ FinCEN, USDA/USFS**

Develop and disseminate a "Common Intelligence Picture." In order to develop a Common Intelligence Picture (CIP), agencies will perform gap analysis of current and emerging products against current and emerging threats. The results of this gap analysis would provide targets for new analytical initiatives. The gap analysis will be comprehensive and centralized. As such, the El Paso Intelligence Center (EPIC), or another existing intelligence capability or program, will be considered the mechanism to support requirements for a "Common Intelligence Picture" for the Northern border. **Action: <u>DOJ/DEA</u>, <u>EPIC</u>, <u>DHS/I&A</u>, DHS/CBP, DHS/ICE, DHS/USCG, DOI, DOJ/ATF, DOJ/FBI, DOJ/NDIC, DOJ/OCDETF, DOD, ODNI, ONDCP/HIDTA, Treasury/FinCEN, USDA/USFS**

Dissemination and Access

3. Conduct a baseline assessment of known policies for the dissemination of counternarcotics intelligence to U.S. Federal, state, local, tribal, and Canadian law enforcement officials, assess for gaps and develop mitigation strategies as warranted.

Assess current information sharing technology systems, and define information flow requirements for meeting expanded sharing of finished intelligence products. Processes and procedures will be established to ensure that intelligence information is shared with or received from Canadian authorities, consistent with applicable laws. **Action: <u>DOJ/DEA</u>, <u>DHS/I&A</u>, DHS/CBP, DHS/ICE, DHS/USCG, DOJ/ATF, DOJ/FBI, DOJ/NDIC, EPIC, DOD, ODNI, ONDCP/HIDTA, Treasury**

Assess current information sharing technology systems and define information flow requirements for meeting expanded sharing of intelligence and law enforcement data sets. Law enforcement and Intelligence Community agencies have been working to enhance information sharing with state, local, and tribal partners along the Northern border. Other partners could include the National Park Service and U.S. Forest Service, as well as law enforcement personnel operating in Indian country, to include the Bureau of Indian Affairs. Such efforts will continue as resources are available, with the goal of expanding the scope, quality, and timeliness of actionable information and to maximize intelligence sharing with appropriate non-Federal entities. Efforts will focus on enhancing and better coordinating existing operations including but not limited to EPIC, the Organized Crime Drug Enforcement Task Force Fusion Center, State and Major Urban Area Fusion Centers, IBETs, BESTs, DEA Task Forces, Bulk Cash Smuggling Center (BCSC), and High Intensity Drug Trafficking Areas (HIDTAs) along the Northern border, as well as information sharing systems such as: Homeland Secure Data Network, Homeland Security Information Network, Law Enforcement Information Sharing Service, Law Enforcement Online (LEO/FBI), EPIC National Seizure System (NSS), National Virtual Pointer System (NVPS), Open Source Center, and the Regional Information Sharing System (RISS). **Action: <u>DOJ/DEA</u>, <u>DHS/I&A</u>, DHS/CBP, DHS/ICE, DHS/USCG, DOI, DOI/BIA, DOJ/ATF, DOJ/FBI, DOJ/NDIC, DOJ/OCDETF, EPIC, ODNI, ONDCP/HIDTA, Treasury, USDA/USFS**

Review and assess existing policies for dissemination and sharing of intelligence and law enforcement data sets, as well as finished intelligence products. Agencies should ensure that an adequate level of education and awareness is established and maintained to emphasize the safeguarding and prevention of the unauthorized disclosure of intelligence. This education includes, but is not limited to, policies regarding security classifications and markings, designation authorities, general handling procedures, dissemination and access, storage, transmission, destruction, and incident reporting. **Action: <u>DOJ/DEA</u>, DOD/ USNORTHCOM, DHS/CBP, DHS/ICE, DHS/I&A, DHS/USCG, DOJ/FBI, DOJ/NDIC, EPIC, ODNI/OSC, ONDCP/HIDTA, Treasury**

4. Coordination and deconfliction of Northern border counternarcotics intelligence.

Coordinate and deconflict Northern border counternarcotics intelligence. A bi-national system of protocols will be established to include uniform deconfliction mechanisms among law enforcement agencies operating along both sides of the border that capitalize upon existing mechanisms in order to prevent duplication of effort, avoid

HIDTAs with Geographic Proximity to the Northern Border	
Chicago HIDTA	New England HIDTA
Lake County HIDTA	New York/New Jersey HIDTA
Michigan HIDTA	Northwest HIDTA
Midwest HIDTA	Ohio HIDTA
Milwaukee HIDTA	Rocky Mountain HIDTA

operational overlap, miscommunication, and minimize potential operational conflicts. Effective intelligence production management must be ensured to avoid the redundant collection of information and duplication of databases and intelligence products, thereby freeing intelligence analysts to expand production and fill gaps in knowledge. HIDTAs will be committed to performing event and target deconfliction, in addition to analytical case support and drug threat assessments. **Action: <u>DOJ/DEA</u>, DOD, DHS/CBP, DHS/ICE, DHS/I&A, DHS/USCG, DOJ/FBI, DOJ/NDIC, EPIC, ODNI, ONDCP/HIDTA**

Partner with State & Major Urban Area Fusion Centers along the Northern border. Fusion centers with Northern border counternarcotics responsibilities will be provided, based upon available resources, with personnel, secure communications, technical and analytic assistance, training, and other core services. Fusion centers are a tool to coordinate with partners to guard against criminal threats and acts of terrorism and improve two-way information sharing across the nation. **Action: <u>DHS/I&A</u>, <u>DOJ/DEA</u>, DHS/CBP, DHS/ICE, DOI, DOJ/FBI, ODNI, ONDCP/HIDTA, USDA/USFS**

Chapter 2: At and Between the Ports of Entry

Background

CBP and ICE, with their broad authorities specific to the border, are the entities directly responsible for border security. However, a comprehensive approach to securing the border, and by extension, improving national security, relies not on one specific Department or agency, but on a complex interweaving of Federal, state, local, tribal, and territorial assets and personnel. By achieving and maintaining security at our borders, we will be better able to protect North America and safeguard as well as facilitate global travel and commerce. This chapter addresses the actions and operations at and between the POEs along the Northern border. From current efforts to future plans and operations, the U.S. Government is working with its partners to deter and eliminate the illegal flow of narcotics, drug proceeds, and weapons north and south across the Northern border.

CBP facilitates legitimate trade and travel, while protecting our country from the threats of global terrorism, illegal migration, and the introduction of narcotics and other contraband. In addition, CBP protects the U.S. economy by enforcing trade laws, intellectual property rights, and the collection of revenue on goods imported into the United States. Along with the Department of Agriculture, CBP protects our food supply and agricultural industry from pests and disease. Similarly, CBP works with Transportation Security Administration and DOD to increase the security of our airspace. ICE has investigative jurisdiction over all laws governing border control, customs, trade, and immigration. Further, some ICE agents are cross-designated to investigate counternarcotics crimes with a clearly articulable nexus to the United States border in coordination with DEA.

The U.S. Government recognizes that the threat posed by drug traffickers is comparable, whether they are attempting to cross the Northern border (in either direction) at or between POEs. CBP's Office of Field Operations (OFO) and Office of Border Patrol (OBP) work hand-in-hand with their Canadian counterparts

---

U.S. Customs and Border Protection Efforts

Office of Field Operations – OFO employs a layered defense strategy and utilizes personnel, cutting-edge technology and canine detection teams to screen people, vehicles and cargo attempting entry into the United States through designated POEs. Currently, OFO operates 95 land POEs on the U.S.-Canada border including three in Alaska.

Office of Border Patrol – OBP is organized into eight Border Patrol sectors along the Northern border. The Border Patrol applies its capabilities based on risk. By maximizing strategic, operational, and tactical information sharing and through Canadian and domestic partnerships, the Border Patrol increases the likelihood of interdiction and apprehension of cross-border illegal activity.

Office of Air and Marine – OAM operates from 16 locations across the Northern border. OAM utilizes a variety of aircraft and marine vessels to proactively patrol the border and support other law enforcement agencies.

on a daily basis. Through both formal and informal relationships, information is exchanged, targets are identified, and operations are coordinated and conducted, deconflicted through established protocols. These bi-national partnerships are essential in achieving joint security goals.

Infrastructure and Technology

Between the POEs, CBP deploys Unmanned Aerial Systems, Remote Video Surveillance Systems, Mobile Surveillance Systems, hand-held night vision equipment and Unattended Ground Sensors to detect illegal cross-border traffic. At the POEs, CBP uses Vehicle and Cargo Inspection Systems, portable back-scatter contraband detectors ("BUSTER"), "Itemiser3" Particle Detection Systems and fiber optic scopes to detect contraband. The use of these technologies enhances CBP's ability to detect contraband and minimizes the need for additional personnel.

Information and Intelligence Sharing

Law enforcement personnel from DHS and DOJ, recognizing that information sharing is a critical component of securing the Northern border, participate in multi-agency, bi-national taskforces and intelligence sharing units. Through close coordination and integration with our Canadian partners and working within established protocols and current MOUs between U.S. and Canadian law enforcement, we can effectively "widen the border" and create a "defense in depth" for both countries by not only interdicting persons or contraband illegally entering or exiting the United States, but also through investigating the TCOs engaged in illicit trade, travel, and finance. By so doing, Canadian and U.S. law enforcement officers are provided with advanced warning to intercept or deter criminal activity.

Field Offices regularly develop special operations in coordination with area ports based on current intelligence trends and analysis developed by the Tactical Analytical Units (TAUs) or other intelligence units and in cooperation/coordination with the Intelligence Community. Many of these special operations focus on current threat analysis that includes inbound/outbound narcotics and currency smuggling and are conducted in a pulse and surge fashion in order to maximize their effect.[10]

In December 2001, Canada created the Canadian National Risk Assessment Centre (NRAC) as the counterpart to the National Targeting Center in the United States. The NRAC has been a critical part of CBP's and CBSA's efforts to meet common goals and allows for information sharing between the two centers on a regular and recurring basis.

Supporting Actions

1. Enhance U.S. Government capabilities at and between the POEs.

Use Information Sharing and risk assessment to drive U.S. Government border management on the Northern border. Real time exchange of information with our partners, both within the U.S. and across the border, can only enhance the Government's ability to effectively secure the borders, while facilitating the flow of legitimate trade and revenue. **Action: <u>DHS</u>, <u>DOJ</u>, DOD, DHS/CBP, DHS/ICE, DHS/USCG**

---

10. Pulse and surge are random, short duration operations designed to saturate an inspection area. The operations are normally unannounced, and utilize officers from different sections to augment the operation.

Pursue Intelligence-Driven Special Operations (IDSO). Intelligence-driven special operations are enforcement operations based on tactical/actionable information. Concentrating future enforcement operations on tactical intelligence will increase the detection and interdiction capabilities of the POEs. **Action: DHS/CBP, DHS/ICE, DOJ/DEA**

Enhance Tactical Analytical Units (TAU),CBP Intelligence Officers [(CBPO(I)], and Field Office Unit program development and further their use when appropriate. TAUs collect and disseminate actionable intelligence, and identify local trends to generate special counternarcotics operations in concert with partner law enforcement agencies to ensure deconfliction. In addition to this analytical work, TAUs continue their outreach efforts and develop relationships with other law enforcement and intelligence teams. CBPO(I) positions are a critical TAU component. These officers provide regional intelligence support to the Field Offices by collecting, analyzing, and disseminating intelligence information to the TAUs and other intelligence components for further exploitation. These relationships provide CBP with access to other agencies' systems and databases which are useful for CBP counternarcotics enforcement operations. **Action: DHS/CBP**

Effectively and efficiently integrate the new Operational Integration Center (OIC) in U.S. Government Northern border management. CBP recently opened and staffed an OIC within the area of responsibility (AOR) of the Detroit Field Office/Detroit Border Patrol Sector. CBP will work directly with other components, to include other Federal agencies and state, local, tribal, and Canadian authorities, to provide real-time situational awareness in their AOR. When permanently funded and jointly staffed, this OIC will be the informational platform that will assist with sharing tactical information in order to identify/intercept violations along the Northern border (smuggling of narcotics, illegal aliens, and currency). Involving our law enforcement partners and providing the real time exchange of information and monitoring of the above stated information will provide a faster and proactive approach to real time emergencies and/or other developing law enforcement situations. **Action: DHS/CBP, DHS/ICE, DHS/USCG, DOJ/DEA, DOJ/FBI**

Enhance current and future participation in task forces and intelligence groups. The continued and expanded participation of law enforcement personnel in intelligence groups and task forces will ensure enhanced cooperation with other law enforcement partners at international, Federal, state, local, and tribal levels. This enhanced cooperation will also ensure the continued exchange of information with our law enforcement partners. **Action: DHS/ICE, DOJ/DEA, DOJ/OCDETF, ONDCP/ HIDTA, DOD, DHS/USCG, DHS/CBP, DOI, DOJ/FBI, DOJ/USMS, DOS, IC, Treasury, USDA/USFS**

Optimize Federal assistance to state and local law enforcement partners where economically effective and feasible. The U.S. Government will formalize a program that encourages interested state, local, tribal, and territorial law enforcement personnel to co-locate with Federal assets where beneficial. This partnership will not only increase the connection between the entities, but experience has shown co-location to be an efficient and effective way to develop force multipliers and share information. Federal agencies and state and local law enforcement agencies may request limited-duration, militarily unique support from the Department of Defense, on a reimbursable and non-reimbursable basis, in authorized mission areas for active duty military forces and National Guard counterdrug support in state status to support counter-drug activities. **Action: <u>DHS/ICE</u>, <u>DOJ/DEA</u>, <u>DOJ/OCDETF</u>, <u>ONDCP/ HIDTA</u>, DOD, DHS/USCG, DHS/CBP, DOI, DOJ/FBI, DOJ/USMS, DOS, IC, USDA/USFS,**

2. Increase the interdiction rates of narcotics and drug proceeds crossing the Northern border.

Work with bi-lateral interagency bodies to further evolve cooperative and integrated border management. In the light of the success of IBET, BEST, and DEA Task Forces, as well as the promise of ICMLEO ShipRider, it is imperative to advance existing cross-border integrated law enforcement initiatives. Integrated cross-border law enforcement is an area where all levels of law enforcement can improve border security and enhance trade, ensuring they are mutually beneficial as part of the cooperative operational measures. **Action: <u>DHS</u>, DOD, DHS/CBP, DHS/ICE, DHS/USCG, DOJ/DEA**

3. Support research and development of counterdrug technologies for deployment at and between POEs.

Further integrate technology and infrastructure advancements at remote and non-remote POEs. Advancement in border management technology will help improve the equipment and infrastructure available to all U.S. Government personnel in the field. Implementing technology or improving existing technology will exponentially improve U.S. Government border management and provide interoperable communications. **Action: <u>DHS/CBP</u>, <u>DHS/S&T</u>**

4. Work toward operational fusion with our Canadian law enforcement partners.

Achieve operational fusion with Canadian partners in interoperable communications, technology, and activities. The ability to integrate Canadian and U.S. technology, including sensors, videos, radio communications, and radar feeds, will permit automated sharing of timely information and will result in more successful counternarcotics enforcement while expediting legitimate trade and travel. **Action: <u>DHS/CBP</u>, DHS/ICE, DHS/USCG, DOJ/DEA**

5. Bring border community members into the counternarcotics mission and adopt a whole of community approach to counternarcotics enforcement.

Adopt a whole-of-community approach to community resilience, including demand reduction efforts. The U.S. Government must work to strengthen and expand its existing partnerships to stifle and eliminate the illicit production, flow, and distribution of narcotics. The U.S.–Canada relationship already supports successful bi-national and multi-agency task forces, but it must work to improve these entities with limited resources. Law enforcement agencies must reach out to community coalitions to develop effective prevention, treatment, and law enforcement partnerships. **Action: <u>ONDCP</u>, DHS/CBP, DHS/ICE, DHS/USCG, DOJ/DEA**

Further integrate community members in border management in and around remote ports of entry. Because most of the Northern border is remote and sparsely populated, U.S. law enforcement will work to bring border residents into some aspects of the border security mission. Northern border residents can serve as law enforcement's eyes and ears in remote areas. Through effective messaging and outreach, border residents learn the vital role they play and the vested interest they have in border security. The inclusion of border residents into a "border-wide community watch" leverages limited law enforcement resources. **Action: <u>DHS/CBP</u>, DHS/ICE, DHS/USCG, DOJ/DEA**

Chapter 3: Air and Marine

Background

Security along the U. S. and Canada's unique land, air, and maritime border is challenged by a variety of shared threats, including drug trafficking. The difficult terrain and extreme winter weather allows for ease of movement by TCOs.

The uniqueness of the border region offers ample methods for TCOs to traffic illicit drugs. For example, TCOs exploit the mountain valleys in Washington and Idaho and coulees in Montana, while the waterways bordering the United States and Canada, when frozen, offer opportunities to move contraband across the international border during the winter months. Spanning 1,500 miles along the Northern border, the Great Lakes form a long, mostly rural coastline, allowing discrete access by vessel and an easy avenue for exploitation by TCOs. During the warmer months, vessels often travel undetected across the international maritime border and make landfall and return, some without reporting into CBP as required.

River areas along the border are exploited by individuals and TCOs. Due to the narrow width of many rivers, a smuggler can quickly travel across the international border and make landfall on the opposite side within seconds of departure. When detected, the smuggler often escapes apprehension by crossing the international border before interdiction can be made. In the winter months, snowmobiles and vehicles are used to transport contraband over frozen rivers and lakes and across the Northern border.

Fundamentally reducing the flow of illicit drugs, drug proceeds, and associated instruments in the air and maritime domains requires a better and more detailed understanding of the flow of these goods. Measuring interdiction rates and impacts of operational efforts requires a clearer understanding of the overall flow of illicit goods in order to assess impacts on that flow resulting from operational interventions. Efforts to develop a reliable methodology for estimating the availability of the four major drug types (cocaine, heroin, marijuana, and meth) are ongoing. To date, estimates developed are useful in assessing trends, but are not yet precise enough to inform performance monitoring.

Supporting Actions:

Enhance Air and Maritime domain awareness and ability to respond along the Northern border.

Increase presence and effectiveness of traditional air and marine domain response capabilities. DHS has increased the number of air and marine assets along the Northern border to enhance detection and response capabilities. Utilizing fixed wing, rotary wing, and UAS assets along with marine assets, CBP/OAM, and the USCG combine efforts and resources to provide the specialized detection and response capabilities necessary to increase border security along the vast expanses of the Northern border. Data gathered from these assets feed into the CBP Air and Marine Operations Center (AMOC), which provides real-time information on detected suspect targets to responders at the Federal, state, and local levels.

These efforts will continue to mature and increase the air and marine response capability along the Northern border.

Recently, CBP and USCG signed Standard Operating Procedures (SOPs) for Coordinated Air and Maritime Operations in the Great Lakes Region that provides a useful model that will be strengthened. Future efforts to strengthen this effort, including the integration and linkage with investigative agencies, DOJ partners and other regional forums will have significant benefits in dealing with a significant portion of the maritime border with Canada that comprises the Great Lakes region. **Action: DHS/CBP, DHS/ USCG, DOD, DHS/ICE**

Enhance interoperable capabilities to increase domain awareness. Seamless and interoperable capability is critical to success. Technology and resources will be prioritized to ensure interoperable communications, encourage collocation of personnel and assets, and foster integrated operations. AMOC creates a comprehensive picture of the air environment in the United States and must be leveraged with any deployment of detection technology along the Northern border as it is the only law enforcement entity that monitors violations of U.S. airspace, track potentially dangerous aircraft, and coordinate and direct an operational response. We must expand these capabilities in order to monitor the border, communicate with our partners, cooperatively act to identify and mitigate potential threats and minimize vulnerabilities, thereby enhancing the ability of the United States to disrupt illegal activity.

Airspace access is a key requirement to CBP's growing fleet of unmanned Predator B aircraft, which operate under Federal Aviation Administration-imposed constraints in geography, altitude, and time of day. These constraints limit their surveillance coverage area, resolution, and sensor options. **Action: DHS/CBP, DHS/ICE, DHS/USCG**

Optimize detection capabilities. DHS has already deployed additional technology to the Northern border, including thermal camera systems, Mobile Surveillance Systems, two UASs and an accompanying Operations Center (UASOC), and Remote Video Surveillance Systems. These technologies integrated into the AMOC enable us to continue to improve our situational awareness in remote areas of the border, and will increase the ability of DHS and partner agencies to detect, deter, and intercept illegal cross-border activity.

Pursuing procurement of commercially available ground-based radar systems, exploring the viability of multi-sensor systems, increasing liaisons with our Canadian partners through Project North Star and the IBETs, and expanding air and marine operations will increase our ability to detect illicit trafficking. Ground-based radar systems could satisfy requirements for closing many of the gaps in the current air surveillance radar coverage. **Action: DHS/CBP, DHS/S&T, DHS/ICE, DHS/USCG, DOJ/USMS**

Integrate Air and Marine Operations Center (AMOC) into the deployment of detection technology. The Air and Marine Operations Center (AMOC) provides a comprehensive situational awareness that is a key to coordinating effective, efficient employment of prosecution assets and to providing officer safety. AMOC has agreements in place that integrate 22 Canadian radar feeds into its operating system to help enhance existing radar coverage gaps and increase the ability to detect, track, and interdict aircraft involved in illicit activity. AMOC must be involved with any deployment of detection technology along the Northern border, as it is the only law enforcement entity that can monitor violations of U.S. airspace, track potentially dangerous aircraft, and coordinate and direct an operational response. Further, AMOC's fused radar picture is a critical component of the U.S. national Common Operational Picture (COP). As AMOC expands, this data needs to be funneled routinely into the strategic domain picture. **Action: DHS/CBP, DHS/S&T, DHS/USCG**

Enhance cooperative U.S. – Canada air and maritime efforts. To enhance domain awareness and interoperability, DHS and its counterparts must utilize interoperable communications systems, collocation of personnel and assets, and joint planning and execution of integrated operations and investigations. CBP will continue to coordinate with the USCG, DEA, and RCMP during planned counternarcotics smuggling operations, law enforcement cross-border operations involving hot pursuit of a suspect, and suspect aircraft tracking. The AMOC has agreements in place that integrates twenty-two Canadian radar feeds into its operating system to help enhance existing radar coverage gaps and increase the ability to detect, track, and interdict aircraft involved in illicit activity. **Action: DHS/CBP, DOD, DHS/ICE, DHS/USCG, DOJ/DEA, DOS, EPIC**

Increase coordination between U.S. and Canadian operations centers to mitigate the use of aircraft and vessels by TCOs. To mitigate the use of aircraft and vessels to move illegal narcotics across the U.S., DHS works closely with the RCMP National Operations Center and interagency partners to optimize their joint operational planning and support efforts during counter-drug operations. In the maritime domain, USCG Operations Integration Center (OIC) initiatives will help sustain a shared awareness and seamless response. Similarly, establishing liaison positions within larger regional command centers will facilitate improved interagency awareness and response capabilities. **Action: DHS/CBP, DHS/USCG, DOD, DHS/ICE, DOJ/DEA, DOS, EPIC**

Chapter 4: Tribal Lands

Background

Federally recognized tribes are sovereign governments located within the boundaries of the United States. The existence of these sovereigns is recognized by the U.S. Constitution (*see* Art. 1, Sec. 8) and the U.S. Supreme Court has clarified tribal government status as "domestic dependent nations." There are over sixty miles of the U.S. border which are jurisdictionally "Indian country" where Federal law determines which sovereigns have jurisdiction to arrest and prosecute. Depending on a number of factors, a crime committed in a tribal territory might be prosecutable in Federal, state, and/or tribal court. One attribute of tribal sovereignty recognized by Federal law is the ability for each tribe to establish a police force to enforce tribal law. Tribal law enforcement officers are often cross-deputized to also enforce Federal and/or state laws.

A number of tribes have their reservations, or other types of Indian country jurisdiction, located on or near the border with Canada. Drug smugglers have been known to seek out tribal jurisdictions in order to smuggle illegal drugs into the United States.

Tribes with lands directly adjacent to the border include Bay Mills Indian Community (Michigan), Blackfeet Tribe (Montana), Grand Portage Band of Chippewa (Minnesota), Red Lake Band of Chippewa (Minnesota), Sault Ste. Marie Chippewa Tribe (Michigan), and St. Regis Mohawk Tribe (New York).

Other Federally recognized tribes have lands located on the shores of one of the Great Lakes or have lands that the lie

> ### Enhanced Coordination Efforts
>
> Enhanced security along the Northern Border relies upon cooperative efforts not only between U.S. and Canadian law enforcement organizations, but between U.S. and tribal law enforcement as well. Cooperation between U.S. Customs and Border Protection and the Blackfeet Nation Homeland Security Program is a prime example of this type of successful coordination. The success of CBP's and the Blackfeet Nation's efforts are the direct result of information sharing, de-confliction efforts, cooperative training, and continuous communication. Reaching beyond cooperative law enforcement efforts to increase this partnership, CBP has participated in the tribal Emergency Response Committee and the Montana Indian Nations working group. The efficacy of these efforts is attributable to the support of the Tribal Council, the leadership of the Director of the Blackfeet Nation Homeland Security Program, the understanding that the threat to the Homeland is real, and that partnerships increase border security and save lives.

within close proximity of the Canadian border, include Aroostook Band of Micmac (Maine), Bad River Band of Lake Superior Chippewa (Wisconsin), Boise Forte Band of Chippewa (Minnesota), Confederated Tribes of the Colville Reservation (Washington), Fort Belknap Indian Community (Montana), Fort Peck Assiniboine & Sioux Tribes (Montana), Houlton Band of Maliseet (Maine), Jamestown S'Klallam Tribe (Washington), Kalispel Tribe (Washington), Keweenaw Bay Indian Community (Michigan), Kootenai Tribe (Idaho), Lower Elwha Klallam Tribe (Washington), Lummi Nation (Washington), Makah Tribe (Washington), Nooksack Tribe (Washington), Passamaquoddy Tribe (Maine), Penobscot Nation (Maine), Red Cliff Band of Lake Superior Chippewa (Wisconsin), Seneca Nation (New York), Swinomish Tribe

(Washington), Tonawanda Seneca Tribe (New York), Turtle Mountain Band of Chippewa (North Dakota), Tuscarora Nation (New York), and Upper Skagit Tribe (Washington).

Criminal jurisdiction on tribal lands is governed by principles of Federal law. Greatly oversimplified, tribes typically exercise jurisdiction over misdemeanors committed by Native Americans. States have jurisdiction over crimes committed by non-Native Americans (unless the victim of the crime was Native American). The Federal Government usually has jurisdiction to prosecute major felony crimes such as murder, aggravated assaults, sexual assaults, and kidnapping pursuant to 18 U.S.C. 1153. There is Federal jurisdiction for crimes committed by non- Native Americans against Native American victims per 18 U.S.C. 1152. Federal crimes of general applicability such as illegally crossing the border or drug smuggling are Federal crimes whether they occur in Indian country or not.

In some tribal jurisdictions, such as on reservations in New York State, the state has been authorized to exercise criminal jurisdiction.

Challenges at St. Regis Mohawk

The St. Regis Mohawk Tribe is a Federally recognized tribe whose reservation lies within the State of New York. Much of the northern border of the reservation is the St. Lawrence River which is coterminous with the U.S.-Canada border. In the river, there are a number of islands which are in the Canadian province of Ontario; these islands are also tribal lands for the Mohawk Council of Akwesasne. The Canadian tribe also has lands south of the river in the province of Quebec which lie adjacent to the U.S. border and the St. Regis Mohawk Tribe's reservation. In other words, the boundaries of seven governments (two countries, two tribes, two provinces, and one state) come together in the same geographical area. To further complicate things, the river often freezes over during the winter resulting in numerous unofficial "ice roads" between the United States and Canada. This unusual intersection of governmental authority of multiple sovereigns and geographical complexity has created an opportunity for criminals seeking to smuggle narcotics into the United States. This area poses unique challenges for the DEA, CBP, ICE, Saint Regis Mohawk Tribal Police, and state and local law enforcement agencies. Inter-jurisdictional cooperation has been a key tool in efforts to interdict narcotics smuggling across Saint Regis Mohawk tribal lands.

Law Enforcement Activity on Tribal Lands

Because of the tripartite division of law enforcement responsibility, a reservation may be patrolled by some combination of Federal, tribal, and/or state law enforcement officers. Despite the number and variety of law enforcement agencies that may have authority to provide services in Indian country, many tribal communities find that there are inadequate law enforcement resources available. Due to this dearth of resources, a number of law enforcement agencies have discovered that pooling resources and working together results in a force multiplier effect and sets the stage for more effective policing, including enforcement of laws prohibiting the smuggling of illegal drugs. Law enforcement officers serving in tribal territories are sometimes cross-deputized to enforce the laws of overlapping jurisdictions and multi-jurisdictional task forces are becoming increasingly common. Each reservation is unique, and great care will be taken to ensure all key players, including tribal law enforcement agencies, are involved in such cooperation.

Criminal Intelligence Information Sharing

Another way law enforcement agencies in Indian country coordinate resources is by sharing criminal intelligence. For example, the St. Regis Mohawk Tribal Police directly participate in information sharing efforts through the New York State Intelligence Center (NYSIC), the regional intelligence fusion center, and EPIC.

Supporting Actions

Enhance coordination of intelligence and law enforcement resources between tribal, Federal, state, and local agencies. While Indian country criminal jurisdiction is fragmented and law enforcement resources are stretched thin, it is imperative that Federal, tribal, state, and local efforts be coordinated. By pooling resources through existing task forces and the efficient sharing of criminal intelligence through intelligence centers, maximum results can be achieved to improve public safety on tribal lands lying on or near the Northern border. Inclusion of tribal law enforcement agencies in Northern border counternarcotic task forces and intelligence centers is crucial, not only to protect tribal communities, but also to protect our nation as a whole from narcotics smuggling from Canada. **Action: DOI/BIA, DHS/CBP, DHS/ICE, DOJ, DOJ/DEA, DOJ/FBI**

Enhance consultation between Federal law enforcement agencies and tribal governments. Federal law enforcement agencies will consult with the tribal governments they serve regarding law enforcement concerns and issues within the tribal communities in order to identify and provide the resources necessary to develop programs that effectively serve the public safety needs of tribal communities. **Action: DOI/BIA, DHS/CBP, DHS/ICE, DOJ, DOJ/DEA, DOJ/FBI**

Develop resources and provide training opportunities to tribal law enforcement agencies. Based on information received from tribal governments about law enforcement needs, Federal agencies will identify and develop resources and provide training opportunities to assist tribal law enforcement agencies, such as the Saint Regis Mohawk Tribal Police, to obtain adequate equipment and personnel to allow full participation in interdiction and enforcement efforts. Depending on identified need, resources might be directed to focus on such things as improving tribal police capability to provide marine patrol services and to more fully participate in criminal intelligence information sharing opportunities. **Action: DOI/BIA, DHS/CBP, DHS/ICE, DOJ, DOJ/DEA, DOJ/FBI**

Chapter 5: Investigations and Prosecutions

Background

U.S. law enforcement benefits from a robust, positive, and close partnership with Justice Canada, the RCMP, and our other law enforcement counterparts in the Government of Canada. Prosecutors and investigators have worked cooperatively on related investigations for many years. The DOJ's Office of International Affairs and its counterpart, Justice Canada's International Assistance Group, facilitate extradition requests and evidence-sharing between the two countries on both Federal, state, and local investigations and prosecutions.

The FBI, DEA, ATF, ICE and USMS have also worked cooperatively with the RCMP and other provincial police authorities. Cooperative cross-border prosecutions allow both partners to share resources, intelligence, and evidence more efficiently. These judicial efforts also help to narrow the enforcement gap by utilizing various U.S. Federal long-arm statutes to indict and prosecute members of Canadian TCOs that intend to ship various drugs into the United States.

Addressing the flow of narcotics across the Northern border can be accomplished by targeting and attacking the criminal organizations responsible. Successful investigations and prosecutions, as well as cooperation and coordination between the U.S. and Canadian governments and law enforcement entities are essential to achieve an effective counternarcotics strategy on the Northern border.

Supporting Actions

1. Increase judicial cooperation with Canada

Improve Information-Sharing and Extradition Processes. Although the United States and Canada have long had a strong law enforcement relationship, there are issues related to cross-border information sharing in the law enforcement context. A fresh look at information- sharing practices under existing mechanisms is necessary, as suggested by the BTB initiative. Under this initiative, the countries will work to promote increased informal sharing of law-enforcement information and evidence, where possible, through police channels and/or among prosecutors.

Steps will also be taken on both sides of the border to expedite and/or streamline the sharing of information and evidence through the MLAT, including third-party or government-generated records. Finally, as stated in the BTB initiative, we will continue working with our Canadian partners to improve the extradition process, including expediting the extradition of fugitives between the two countries. **Action: DOJ/OIA, DHS/CBP, DHS/ICE, DOJ/DEA, DOJ/FBI, DOJ/USMS, DOS**

Increase the capabilities of law enforcement investigative agencies to obtain information from electronic communication service providers. Both the U.S. and Canada have demanding legal requirements governing law enforcement access to electronic communications and related records, and sharing such information pursuant to current agreements and practices has at times been difficult and slow. These problems have been exacerbated as TCOs and criminal enterprises have switched to secure encrypted communication providers to shield their illegal communications from law enforcement detection. In order to determine the leaders and organizers of these organizations and to obtain timely information about the movement of drugs, money, and the criminals themselves, it is imperative that Canada and the United States work together to expedite the sharing of information from electronic communication service providers; and share information necessary to lay the foundation for intercepting internet and voice communications under their respective laws in a timely manner. **Action: <u>DOJ/DEA</u>, DHS/ICE, DOJ/FBI, DOJ/OIA, DOJ/USMS, DOS**

Develop and implement an expedited system for obtaining financial records and freezing and forfeiting assets. In order to disrupt and dismantle the most significant TCOs operating along the Northern border, investigations and prosecutions must attack the entire financial infrastructure of the targeted organizations and destroy their ability to operate. Recognizing that TCOs' financial infrastructures are international in nature, it is essential to have a full and complete financial investigation, including identifying and tracing the flow of the unlawful proceeds, in order for the TCOs' assets to be frozen and ultimately forfeited. Although there are legal mechanisms in place for obtaining such assistance, those mechanisms, including our bilateral MLAT, are often too slow. The United States and Canada should develop new protocols to expedite the MLAT process to obtain financial records and freeze and seize TCO assets, as well as identify more informal information exchanges that can facilitate financial investigations and asset seizures. FIUs have information exchange systems in place to obtain financial intelligence to support the freezing and forfeiture of assets, and these protocols should be utilized and evaluated for effectiveness. Further, most of the Canadian provinces recognize non-conviction based forfeiture, although Federal law in Canada does not. The United States and Canada will work together to encourage and formalize referrals to the provincial level in non-conviction based forfeiture cases, where appropriate. **Action: <u>DOJ</u>, DHS/ICE, DOJ/DEA, DOJ/FBI, DOJ/USMS, DOS, Treasury/FinCEN, Treasury/IRS, Treasury/OFAC**

Improve Cooperation in Undercover Operations and Sensitive Investigative Tactics. Cross-border undercover operations are critical tools in counternarcotics investigations. Recognizing differences in U.S. and Canadian criminal law is imperative in order to define the legal parameters in which to use confidential sources, conduct international controlled deliveries or controlled money pick-ups, conduct monitored phone calls into Canada from the United States and obtain wiretaps in Canada. Once the legal parameters have been established, a process to obtain the necessary legal approvals in the U.S. and Canada will be developed that is both timely and efficient. Additionally, efforts should be made to increase the availability of reciprocal resources between the United States and Canada, to include the ability to acquire and use backstopping methods for U.S. law enforcement operating in Canada. **Action: <u>DOJ/DEA</u>, <u>DOJ/OIA</u>, <u>DHS/ICE</u>, DOJ/FBI, DOJ/USMS, DOS**

2. Address the production of Canadian narcotics.

Use Joint and Coordinated efforts among U.S. and Canadian Law Enforcement Agencies to Disrupt and Dismantle Canadian Marijuana and Ecstasy Production. Identifying and dismantling the criminal enterprises responsible for producing high-grade marijuana and Ecstasy is imperative. Improved investigative collaboration and coordination between key U.S. and Canadian law enforcement agencies and task forces will increase the ability of the U.S. and Canadian governments to attack the commercial operations and financial infrastructures of these major TCOs, while also enhancing criminal investigations and prosecutions. **Action: <u>DOJ/DEA</u>, DHS/CBP, DHS/ICE, DOJ/FBI**

Develop enforcement capacity and regulatory frameworks to address precursor chemicals. Canada's continued role as a source country for Ecstasy to U.S. markets highlights the need for greater cooperation in tracking precursor chemical activity. The United States looks forward to future engagement with Canada to build coordinated enforcement capacity and regulatory frameworks to promote industry compliance and avoid diversion of precursor chemicals and laboratory equipment for criminal use. In addition, the United States will work with Canada to more aggressively curb the rise of methamphetamine production. **Action: <u>DOJ/DEA</u>, DHS/CBP, DHS/ICE, DOJ/FBI**

3. Increase investigative and task force resources.

Optimize prosecutorial support to Northern border districts. The U.S. Government will take steps to more efficiently use current capabilities of not only the source districts, but also the Northern border districts where the cross border drug trade is occurring. These resources will include both Organized Crime Drug Enforcement Task Force (OCDETF) and non-OCDETF Assistant U.S. Attorney positions. Equally important is the need to optimize the agent workforce in the Northern border investigative regions. OCDETF regions and districts recognize these threats and are investigating and prosecuting reactive cases as well as pursuing proactive initiatives to combat this problem. **Action: <u>DOJ</u>, DHS/ICE/CBP, DOJ/DEA, DOJ/FBI**

Encourage agency participation in the OCDETF, HIDTA, DEA Task Forces, IBET, and BEST programs. The OCDETF program has a strategy to identify and track Consolidated Priority Organization Targets (CPOTs). The CPOT program seeks to identify the current, most prolific drug traffickers in the world and direct resources towards their prosecution and apprehension, as well as the disruption and dismantlement of their organizations. The HIDTA program reduces drug availability by assisting Federal, state, local, and tribal law enforcement agencies to dismantle and disrupt transnational criminal organizations. The BEST, IBET, and DEA Task Force programs provide a bi-national investigative and interdiction platform in which U.S. and Canadian law enforcement officers investigate and interdict transnational criminal organizations who exploit the Northern border. The OCDETF, HIDTA, IBET, BEST, and DEA Task Force programs will provide various training forums and seminars to enhance cooperative U.S. Government efforts. **Action: <u>DHS/CBP, DHS/ICE, DOJ/DEA, DOJ/FBI, DOJ/OCDETF, ONDCP/HIDTA</u>**

Coordinate with DEA's Special Operations Division (SOD). SOD is a multi-agency, DEA-led operational coordination center which serves as the nucleus for focusing DEA, FBI, ICE, and numerous other participating Federal law enforcement, intelligence, and investigative resources on key command and control nodes of international TCOs. SOD has the ability to collect, analyze, deconflict, and disseminate operational information and intelligence derived from worldwide multi-agency sources, including classified projects. SOD converts sensitive information into usable leads and tips which are passed to the field for real-time enforcement activity against major international criminal enterprises. Coordinating with SOD will ensure U.S. cases with multi-district and international reach are conducted in concert to maximize the disruptive impact to illegal drug activity. **Action: <u>DOJ/DEA</u>, DHS/ICE/CBP, DOJ/FBI**

4. Target the financial infrastructure of TCOs.

Optimize the Capabilities of Investigative and Financial Regulatory Agencies, U.S. Attorneys Offices, and Canadian Prosecutors to Dismantle the Financial Infrastructure of Northern border TCOs. The monetary proceeds from the illegal distribution of Canadian high-potency marijuana and Ecstasy are funneled to the TCOs through bulk cash smuggling over the Northern border and through the use of Money Services Businesses (MSB). TCOs use MSBs to move drug trafficking proceeds from the U.S. to Canada and other countries to reimburse sources of supply, invest in legitimate and criminal activities, and support family members. Such money transactions are often structured to avoid reporting requirements and law enforcement attention.

Regulatory efforts should be coordinated to ensure compliance with Anti-Money Laundering (AML) procedures and reporting requirements for tracking proceeds of crime while still allowing for legitimate economic activity. Efforts should be made to ensure compliance by all money transmitters and appropriate civil and criminal enforcement against unlicensed money transmitters.

Investigations and prosecutions must attack the entire financial infrastructure of the targeted organizations in order to destroy their ability to operate. Law enforcement will seek to focus existing resources on the coordinated and strategic use of money laundering/bulk cash smuggling prosecutions with asset forfeiture together with all other strategic and tactical methods to prevent the cross-border movement of illicit proceeds. U.S. law enforcement must continue to develop leads from Suspicious Activity Reports (SARs) as well as increase agent training in financial investigation techniques in order to improve and enhance financial investigations that follow bulk cash interdictions. Oftentimes, bringing these prosecutions under the OCDETF program will provide additional resources to identify and dismantle these criminal organizations. In addition, OCDETF member agencies will train and assist state and local law enforcement at all levels of experience to gain valuable intelligence for investigation development following bulk cash seizures. **Action: DHS/ICE, DOJ, Treasury/IRS, DOJ/DEA, DOJ/FBI, EPIC. Treasury/FinCEN**

Conclusion

The vast 5,225-mile border and evolving drug trafficking trends provide numerous challenges for law enforcement and intelligence entities operating along the Northern border under differing authorities, protocols, and expertise. By enhancing the strong history of partnerships among Federal, state, local, tribal, and Canadian counterparts and building on current effective programs and operations, the United States and Canada will find success in reducing the cross-border flow of illicit drugs. This _Strategy_ provides an overview of current efforts and broad supporting actions aimed at achieving this goal. Above all, through integrated cross-border law enforcement, the United States and Canada will build upon existing relationships, programs and policies; seek further opportunities to pursue national security by disrupting TCO; and improve our information sharing, allowing us to use our resources more efficiently and effectively to curb the flow of illicit drugs and drug proceeds across the Northern border.

The Office of National Drug Control Policy (ONDCP), in coordination with the Department of Homeland Security (DHS), Office of Counternarcotics Enforcement; the Department of Justice (DOJ), Office of the Deputy Attorney General; and the Department of State (DOS), Bureau of Western Hemisphere Affairs, will oversee a comprehensive and transparent implementation process, providing updates on progress toward achieving the *Strategy's* objectives. In addition, the National Northern Border Counternarcotics Strategy supports a comprehensive effort along the Northern border, to include BTB, the 2010 National Drug Control Strategy, the DHS Quadrennial Homeland Security Review (QHSR), individual Federal agency strategies, and other border related efforts and strategies.

Appendix 1: Measuring Progress on the Implementation of the National Northern Border Counternarcotics Strategy

Measuring Progress on the Implementation of the National Northern Border Counternarcotics Strategy

To ensure effective implementation of the *National Northern Border Counternarcotics Strategy* and progress toward the Administration's *National Drug Control Strategy* goal of curtailing illicit drug consumption in the U.S., it is critical to have indicators that will enable status tracking of the *Strategy's* implementation. Provided below are measurable indicators corresponding to the five strategic objectives of the *Northern Border Counternarcotics Strategy*. While progress reports on the *Strategy* will include narratives highlighting successes and identifying challenges in more detail, including current resource limitations, the intent is to provide a consolidated list of indicators, one per objective, which provides a "dashboard" indicating the extent of progress in pursuing the strategic goal. These indicators are not comprehensive, nor illustrative of each chapter, but they do provide an "at a glance" indication of our progress in some of the most crucial areas of the *Strategy*. These indicators will provide baseline numbers for future *Strategy* updates.

Strategic Goal

Substantially reduce the flow of illicit drugs and drug proceeds along the Northern border.

Strategic Objectives

Chapter 1: Intelligence and Information Sharing

- Objective: Enhance intelligence and information sharing capabilities and processes associated with the Northern border.

- Indicator: Number of intelligence databases relevant to the Northern border or counternarcotics that the following entities share among each other: Operational Integration Center (OIC), El Paso Intelligence Center (EPIC), Organized Crime Drug Enforcement Task Force (OCDETF) fusion center, Northern border High Intensity Drug Trafficking Areas (HIDTAs), Bulk Cash Smuggling Center (BCSC), and State and Major Urban Area Fusion Centers in the Northern border region

- Objective: Expand intelligence and information sharing among all entities with Northern Border equities.

- Indicator: Numbers of finished intelligence products that address Intelligence Requirements of Key Intelligence Questions in support of Northern Border law enforcement operations.

Chapter 2: At and Between the Ports of Entry

- Objective: Interdict illicit drugs and illicit drug proceeds at and between the ports of entry along the Northern border.

- Indicator: Seizures at and between the border ports of entry in the following categories:

Marijuana	Ecstasy	Cocaine	Heroin	Meth	Bulk Currency	Firearms

Chapter 3: Air and Marine

- Objective: Interdict illicit drugs and illicit drug proceeds in the air and maritime domains along the Northern border.

- Indicator: Seizures along the Northern border and maritime approaches by DHS in the following categories:

Marijuana	Ecstasy	Cocaine	Heroin	Meth	Bulk Currency	Firearms

Chapter 4: Tribal Lands

- Objective: Enhance counterdrug efforts and cooperation with tribal governments along the Northern border.

- Indicator: Number of task forces and intelligence centers on the Northern border with tribal representation and training offered to tribal representatives.

Chapter 5: Investigations and Prosecutions

- Objective: Disrupt and dismantle transnational criminal organizations operating along the Northern border.

- Indicator: Number of U.S. Attorney General's Canada-based Consolidated Priority Organization Targets (CPOTs) and Regional Priority Organization Targets (RPOTs) identified as operating in Canada and/or utilizing the Northern border to further their criminal enterprise.

Appendix 2: Resource Annex

Overview of Funding for the National Northern Border Counternarcotics Strategy

Overview of Funding for the National Northern Border Counternarcotics Strategy

	FY2011 Enacted[1,2] (000)
Intelligence and Information Sharing Efforts	
DHS/U.S. Immigration and Customs Enforcement	1,096
DoJ/National Drug Intelligence Center	109
Subtotal, Intelligence and Sharing	**1,205**
Efforts at and between the Ports of Entry[3]	
DHS/U.S. Customs and Border Protection	224,605
Subtotal, Ports of Entry	224,605
Efforts against Air and Marine threats	
DHS/U.S. Customs and Border Protection	148,220
DHS/U.S. Coast Guard	12,507
DoT/Federal Aviation Administration	456
Subtotal, Air and Marine	**161,183**
Investigations and Prosecutions	
DHS/U.S. Immigration and Customs Enforcement	88,429
DoJ/Criminal Division	2,554
DoJ/Drug Enforcement Administration	164,806
DoJ/Executive Office for U.S. Attorneys	9,792
DoJ/Organized Crime Drug Enforcement Task Force	59,793
DoJ/Office of Federal Detention Trustee	42,225
DoJ/Office of Justice Programs	2,485
DoJ/U.S. Marshals Service	23,724
Subtotal, Investigations and Prosecutions	**393,808**

[1]Estimates for FY 2012 are not included in this annex. Enactment of "The Budget Control Act of 2011", P.L. 112-25, subsequent to the transmission of the President's FY 2012 Budget request to the Congress, has created uncertainty about FY 2012 program funding levels.

[2]The Department of Defense was unable to identify counternarcotics funding devoted solely to the Northern border.

[3]The resources for Tribal Lands are included in the Ports of Entry and Investigations totals.

Department of Homeland Security
U.S. Customs and Border Protection

Program: Office of Border Patrol

FY 2011 Enacted funding level ($ 000): $43,336

Program Description:

The Office of Border Patrol is responsible for protection the homeland by reducing the likelihood that dangerous people and capabilities enter the United States between ports of entry (POEs). These illegal entries include aliens and drug smugglers, potential terrorists, wanted criminals, and persons seeking to avoid inspection at the designated ports of entry due to their undocumented status.

The Border Patrol's fundamental mission is to secure our borders between Ports of Entry (POEs) against all threats, including terrorists and terrorist weapons, Transnational Criminal Organizations (TCOs) and illegal immigration. This strategy calls for the Border Patrol to take a risk-based, outcome-focused approach to achieving this mission. This will be achieved using tools, programs, techniques and approaches that are focused on applying *Information, Integration and Rapid Response* to be more focused, effective and efficient.

CBP has made important security improvements along the Northern border, investing in additional Border Patrol agents, technology and infrastructure. CBP reached a staffing level of 20,679 Border Patrol agents as of December 31, 2010 and plans to hire additional agents in FY 2011 to reach a level of 21,370. Currently, CBP has more than 2,200 Border Patrol agents deployed to the Northern border, a 700 percent increase since 9/11. CBP also has nearly 3,800 CBP Officers managing the flow of people and of goods across the Northern border ports of entry and crossings.

CBP also plans to continue to add to its inventory of tactical infrastructure and technology deployments on the border in FY 2011. In addition, CBP will continue to deploy technology, such as sensors and cameras, to increase the Border Patrol's ability to detect illegal entries and to provide greater situational awareness.

The Border Patrol also uses the Northern Border Resident Agent Program (RAP), Transportation Checks, Tactical Checkpoints, and Joint Operations to gain and maintain control of the border. These are described below:

Resident Agent Program

The Resident Agent Program is a new and innovative approach for the Northern border to extend corridor security by embedding agents into communities that previously had limited Border Patrol presence due to the remoteness of the location. This Border Patrol presence has promoted the establishment of relationships with local law enforcement in the surrounding communities, which previously did not exist. Daily interaction with other agencies and communities have formed trusting relationships, and as a result allowed the shared information to be more timely and precise. As this intelligence is reported up the chain of command it provides the Sector valuable information as the Sector maintains its process of continually evaluating resource alignment and requirements. The Resident Agent Program has been reconfigured from a singular focus and tactical approach of improving defense-in-depth capabilities and refocused towards expanding situational awareness within the sector. Resident Agents are ideally suited for providing the field commanders with an unprecedented level of situational awareness within interior areas of the border. Resident Agents are able to provide improved situational awareness by focusing their daily activities on the creation of partnerships, expansion of community outreach, and the development and dissemination of intelligence. This situational awareness is leveraged to benefit DHS, and CBP's Border Patrol Sectors, Field Offices, and Air and Marine Branches.

Transportation Checks

Transportation checks at critical transit nodes have become an integral part of day-to-day Northern border operations. Significant numbers of aliens from special interest countries have been located, identified, arrested, and subsequently removed from the U.S. as a direct result of successful transportation check operations. Additionally, intelligence gained from transportation checks has proven to be an effective tool for agent deployment along the Southern border. Northern border sectors are expected to continue current transportations check duties and expand these activities as manpower and operations permit.

Tactical Checkpoints

Tactical checkpoints are another enforcement tool, which has proven effective along the Northern border when deployed properly. Tactical checkpoints have been especially useful when utilized in regions where other traditional patrol methods pose an officer safety concern, such as in New York State on the roads leading from the Akwesasne Reservation. As manpower and current threat pictures evolve, tactical checkpoints will remain a strong enforcement tool to be utilized in Northern border sector AORs. Partnering with other law enforcement agencies in checkpoint operations will further enhance operational effectiveness.

Joint Operations

Northern border sectors have a long history of participating in successful joint operations aside from Integrated Border Enforcement Teams (IBET) operations and task forces. Operations and joint patrols with Federal, state, county, tribal, and local law enforcement agencies greatly increase other agency awareness of our mission and ultimately provide sectors with extra eyes and ears in border areas which assist them in gaining greater situational awareness. When used effectively, joint operations and joint patrols are an effective force multiplier strategy. Field commanders are encouraged to promote station level joint operations with other agencies and to strengthen existing partnerships.

The Border Patrol also establishes and maintains effective partnerships, formal and informal, with other Federal, state and local law enforcement agencies, as well as other Federal agencies that have an interest in the border regions. Further, the Border Patrol maintains international partnerships to enhance border security primarily with agencies of the governments of Mexico and Canada. A number of these partnerships are described below.

Integrated Border Enforcement Teams

There are fifteen IBETs in twenty-four locations working in land, air and marine environments between the ports of entry along the U.S./Canada international border. IBETs are traditionally composed of the Royal Canadian Mounted Police (RCMP), Canada Border Services Agency (CBSA), CBP's Border Patrol, the U.S. Coast Guard (USCG) and other Federal, state and local law enforcement agencies. These multi-agency intelligence driven teams augment the integrity and security of the border by identifying, investigating, and interdicting individuals and organizations that pose a threat to the security of both nations. Through continuous collaboration and coordination the IBETs are able to synchronize operations between countries to expand the borders.

Northern Border Integration Demonstration (NBID)/ Operation Integration Center (OIC)

The goals of the NBID project are to provide operational integration of border security efforts in the Detroit area, and enhance the situational awareness for the CBP and all mission partners in the region. Operational integration will be improved by developing and demonstrating an OIC. The first OIC opened March 24, 2011 in Detroit and will provide a collaborative work area and communications capabilities for representatives of all program offices of CBP, other DHS component agencies, Federal law enforcement agencies, state and local law enforcement, and appropriate Canadian agencies. The OIC will be able to support collaboration among as many as 40 on-site personnel from the various participating agencies. This collaboration includes law enforcement intelligence coordination.

State/County/Local Counter Narcotics Task Forces

Members of CBP are assigned to various counternarcotics and counter crime/terrorism task forces. They add a myriad of tools and resources to often times poorly funded and understaffed local agencies. These task forces work on drug and violent crimes associated with narcotics trafficking that affect the border communities and concentrate on a coordinated response to disrupt, dismantle and defeat criminal organizations.

Border Patrol National Native American Program

The mission of the Border Patrol National Native American Program is to facilitate new partnerships, improve relationships, and increase trust throughout the Native American Indian tribes that have a nexus to the U.S. border. The program champions partnerships between tribal law enforcement, various Native American organizations, and the Border Patrol to support the national strategy. The Border Patrol National Native American Program is operational in 12 of the Border Patrol sectors. The program acts as a conduit between the Border Patrol and tribal, local, state and Federal law enforcement agencies, as well as tribal councils located along both the southwest and Northern borders.

The program was designed to support ongoing enforcement operations within the respective agencies, while enhancing the liaison between them. As the relationship solidified, contact and responses to illicit activity along the borders has increased, allowing for joint law enforcement support for both Border Patrol and tribal law enforcement. Routine communication and liaison between some sectors and tribal council officials has led to enhancing the security and safety of the agents who are working in dangerous areas along the border. Through the Border Patrol National Native American Program, information-sharing efforts have allowed the Border Patrol sectors to conduct All-Terrain Vehicle training, search and rescue training, advanced four-wheel-drive training, and vehicle stops.

The Border Patrol National Native American Program is working to standardize policies and procedures and is proactively developing performance measures for the program to evaluate and measure the effectiveness of its initiatives.

Borderlands Management Task Forces (BMTF)

These task forces were created to facilitate an intergovernmental forum for cooperative problem-solving on common issues related to the international border. The primary mission is to address border security, human safety, and natural and cultural resource protection through shared resources, information, communication, problem-solving, standardization, and training. An integral part of the BMTF is the participation of the Sector Public Lands Liaison agents (PLLA).

The PLLA works to foster better communication, increase the interagency understanding of respective mission objectives and priorities, and serve as a central point of contact within the Border Patrol to facilitate the successful resolution of environmental issues at the local level.

FY 2011 Planned accomplishments include:

- Continue to disrupt transnational criminal organizations operating along the border;

- Establish first Operation Integration Center in Detroit, Michigan;

- Increase end of FY 2010 staffing by 859 agents to arrive at an end-state level of 21,370 agents;

- Maintain 2,212 Border Patrol agents along the Northern border;

- Strengthen existing partnerships with local, state, and other Federal agencies;

- Establish Northern Border priority intelligence requirements; and

- Leverage personnel and technology accrued from applying resources more efficiently to reduce the flow of known, illegal cross-border traffic along other areas of the border.

Department of Homeland Security
U.S. Customs and Border Protection

Program: Office of Field Operations

FY 2011 Enacted funding level ($ 000): $164,042

Program Description:

CBP officers and agriculture specialists are multi-disciplined and perform the full range of inspection, intelligence analysis, examination, and law enforcement activities relating to the arrival and departure of persons, conveyances, and merchandise at ports of entry. These enforcement activities prevent the entry of terrorists and instruments of terror, harmful pests and diseases, illegal drugs and contraband, illegal aliens, and importations/exportations contrary to law and trade agreements, from entering/ exiting the U.S.

While the counter smuggling principles employed by CBP at U.S. Northern border POEs are consistent with those employed along the Southwest border, the approach differs drastically from the Southwest border approach. Unlike the Southern border, which is equipped with more personnel and resources, the Northern border approach focuses more on bi-national, Federal, state, local, and tribal law enforcement partnerships, information sharing agreements, joint integrated operations, and community outreach in order to maximize efforts and resources. This approach has proven successful along the Northern border.

Inbound Activities

CBP employs a layered defense strategy and utilizes personnel, cutting-edge technology and canine detection teams to screen people, vehicles and cargo attempting entry into the U.S. through designated POEs. Currently CBP operates 86 land POEs on the U.S.-Canada border including 4 in Alaska.

Surge marina patrols are conducted jointly by CBP, U.S. Immigration and Customs Enforcement (ICE), the USCG, Drug Enforcement Administration (DEA) and state and local authorities during small boat season in order to deter and interdict smuggling operations as well as conduct community outreach to the along the marinas.

Field offices regularly develop special operations in coordination with area ports based on current intelligence trends and analysis developed and reviewed by the Tactical Analytical Units (TAUs) and in cooperation/coordination with the Intelligence Community. Many of these special operations focus on current threat analysis that includes inbound/outbound narcotics and currency smuggling and are conducted in a pulse and surge fashion in order to maximize the effect.

Outbound Activities

CBP recognizes that the threat posed by drug traffickers is the same whether they are attempting to cross the Northern border (north or south). Because of this, CBP works hand-in-hand with Canadian counterparts on a daily basis. Through both formal and informal relationships information is exchanged, targets are identified, and operations are coordinated and conducted. These bi-national partnerships are essential and have proven successful in achieving our joint mission.

CBP employs a "pulse and surge" strategy for outbound operations at most Northern border crossings. "Pulse and surge" operations are short duration but periodic outbound inspections that are followed by periods without inspections. The operations are conducted either randomly and/or are intelligence driven. This allows for immediate stand-down of outbound inspections to manage traffic flow departing the port of entry. The random and/or intelligence implications of this strategy significantly improve the CBP Officers (CBPOs) tactical capability.

FY 2011 Planned accomplishments include:

Deliver a traffic management system (light emitting diodes signage) to the high-volume land POEs, complete deployment of Western Hemisphere Travel Initiative (WHTI) technology, maintain a secure border at the land POEs while facilitating legitimate trade and travel, and extend WHTI facilitative technology to other environments such as pedestrian processing, ferries, and rail;

- The Operational Intelligence Center (OIC) was recently opened in Selfridge, Michigan in order to further facilitate the flow and exchange of tactical and actionable intelligence.; and

- Strengthen established relationships among Federal, state, local, tribal and Canadian Authorities through active participation in IBET is a priority for CBP.

Department of Homeland Security
U.S. Customs and Border Protection

Program: Office of Air and Marine

FY 2011 Enacted funding level ($ 000): $148,220

Program Description:

The Office of Air and Marine (OAM) provides rapid-response surveillance and interdiction capabilities in areas where border enforcement is made difficult due to terrain or location. OAM agents use air and maritime assets to develop and sustain the detection and monitoring, interception, tracking, and apprehension of suspect targets along the Northern border to guard against illegal activity and border violations on the ground, air, or water. OAM provides air and maritime support to OBP, OFO, and its interagency partners including ICE and DEA. Within OAM there are several simultaneous programs that optimize CBP's deterrent and interdiction capabilities along the Northern border:

The Director of Northern Operations has overall situational awareness of 16 Aviation and Marine Units located from Bellingham, Washington to Houlton, Maine spanning over 5,200 miles of international border. The mission is to provide OAM's field directors with the correct aviation and maritime assets, personnel, and operational budget to accomplish their missions. The Director has continuous oversight of: aviation operations, training and evaluation of equipment, personnel and asset relocation, administrative, facilities, budgetary, and disciplinary actions occurring within the region. The OBP Sector Chief has tactical control of OAM assets in the Northern border and all operations are based on the priorities established by OBP.

Air and Marine Operations Center (AMOC)

AMOC detects, tracks and coordinates response activities related to suspect aircraft along the Northern border with other Department of Homeland Security component agencies (U.S. Coast Guard, ICE, OBP), and other Federal, state, and local authorities, as well as with other interagency task forces and with Canadian authorities. The AMOC has a comprehensive depiction of Northern border airports displayed in its reporting system. To better maximize the effectiveness of law enforcement efforts, OAM performs outreach with local law enforcement agencies to provide information on OAM capabilities and available support.

The AMOC has agreements in place that integrates twenty-two Canadian radar feeds into its operating system to help enhance existing radar coverage gaps and increase the ability to detect, track, and interdict aircraft involved in illicit activity. Radar coverage of U.S. maritime approaches, borders, and interior is consolidated at the AMOC. Currently, AMOC relies primarily on feeds from 282 Federal Aviation Administration (FAA) and Department of Defense (DOD) radars to provide a common operating picture (COP) of our air domain. AMOC provides a comprehensive situational awareness that is a key to coordinating effective, efficient employment of prosecution assets and to providing officer safety. This capability is a key requirement of CBP's AMOC Phase B program, which will expand its predominantly air-centric COP into a multi-domain COP. Further, AMOC's fused radar picture is a critical component of the U.S. national COP.

Optimize and enhance detection capabilities

DHS is pursuing procurement of commercially available ground-based radar systems and exploring the viability of proof of concept multi-sensor systems. Additionally, DHS is seeking increased liaisons with our Canadian partners through Project North Star and the IBETs. CBP is expanding air and marine operations on the Northern border, including the deployment of Unmanned Aircraft Systems (UASs). Ground-based radar systems could satisfy requirements for closing many of the gaps in current air surveillance radar coverage. Airborne early warning radar-equipped aircraft at 30,000 to 35,000 feet would extend the nominal 100- nautical miles (nm) horizon of ground radar's coverage to 180+ nm. Aerostats would provide a look-down perspective that would defeat most terrain/urban build-up shadowing as well as extend the curvature-of-the-earth horizon but would suffer to some degree from terrain shadowing due to their lower altitude (10,000 to 14,000 feet), and bad weather would limit their deployment. However, Northern border weather patterns would support 65% aloft times required of tethered arrays, the same percentage as the Southwest border.

DHS has already deployed additional technology to the Northern border, including thermal camera systems, Mobile Surveillance Systems, two UASs and an accompanying Operations Center (UASOC), and Remote Video Surveillance Systems. These technologies enable us to continue to improve our situational awareness in remote areas of the border, and in turn will increase the ability of DHS and partner agencies to detect, deter, and intercept illegal cross-border activity.

Utilizing a vast array of sensors, communications networks, law enforcement, FAA and intelligence databases, and interagency agreements, AMOC has a comprehensive picture of the air environment in the U.S. AMOC must be involved with any deployment of detection technology along the Northern border as it is the only law-enforcement entity that can monitor violations of U.S. airspace, track potentially dangerous aircraft, and coordinate and direct an operational response.

Enhance domain awareness

To enhance domain awareness and interoperability, DHS and its counterparts must utilize interoperable communications systems, collocation of personnel and assets, and joint planning and execution of integrated operations and investigations. Most of the coordination by CBP is accomplished through the RCMP National Operations Center in Ottawa. CBP works with the RCMP on a daily basis for aircraft sorting, coordination on suspect air targets, flight plans inquiries, flight following and pilot informational requests. In addition, CBP coordinates with the RCMP during planned counternarcotics smuggling operations, law enforcement cross-border operations involving hot pursuit of suspects, and the tracking of suspect aircraft.

The diversity of this border environment is unified by one common feature: the partnership and alliance between the U.S. and Canada. If we are to succeed in disrupting Transnational Criminal Organizations (TCOs) operating on the Northern border, we must operate in close conjunction with our Canadian partners. We must continue to formalize partnerships that coordinate efforts to combat TCOs and eliminate procedural and legal frameworks that hinder cooperation.

Department of Homeland Security
U.S. Customs and Border Protection

Program: Border Security Fencing, Infrastructure and Technology

FY 2011 Enacted funding level ($ 000): $3,000

Program Description:

Border Security Fencing, Infrastructure and Technology (BSFIT) funding is issued for technology that provides surveillance and detection support, which improves situational awareness along the land and maritime regions of the Northern border. The projects that deploy the surveillance and detection capabilities fill capability gaps against priority threats in high threat areas. The threats of concern across the Northern border include terrorist activity, drug smuggling, contraband smuggling, human smuggling, and mala fide traveler. Currently, no financial metrics exist to identify the exact cost associated with each of these threats of concern.

FY 2011 Planned accomplishments include:

Replenish resources/assets deployed from the southeast/coastal area to the Northern border in FYs 2008 and 2009 to support the establishment of the final two primary OAM branches in North Dakota and the Great Lakes region of Detroit. This approach represents CBP OAM's deployment end-state that considers the entirety of our Nation's borders and will best address threats and will provide increased efficiencies and operational effectiveness; and

- Continue providing a reasonable level of aviation support along all borders.

Department of Homeland Security
U.S. Customs and Border Protection

Program: Office of Information Technology

FY 2011 Enacted funding level ($ 000): $12,686

Program Description:

Office of Information Technology (OIT) supports the drug enforcement mission through the acquisition, and support, and maintenance of technology, such as non-intrusive inspection (NII) systems, government developed mission critical systems, and processing of cargo and passenger vetting through CBP's and DHS' data centers. These systems provide support across the CBP mission not just drug interdiction. The enforcement activity performed by CBP officers or Border Patrol agents may lead to several end results including drug interaction.

FY 2011 Planned accomplishments include:

Ensure deployed NII technologies meet expected operational requirements of CBP.

Department of Homeland Security
U.S. Customs and Border Protection

Program: Office of Training and Development

FY 2011 Enacted funding level ($ 000): $1,541

Program Description:

The Office of Training and Development (OTD) leads and directs CBP training programs. OTD ensures that all training efforts support the CBP mission and strategic goals, meet the needs of a diverse and geographically dispersed workforce, and contribute to measurable outcomes and results. OTD establishes standards for designing, developing, delivering, and evaluating training. The office directly executes career development programs; basic and advanced training to all occupations; and supervisory, management, and executive development programs via the annual agency-wide training plan.

Department of Homeland Security
U.S. Immigration and Customs Enforcement

Program: Homeland Security Investigations – Domestic Investigations

FY 2011 Enacted funding level ($ 000): $88,049

Program Description:

ICE is a multi-mission investigative law enforcement agency; within ICE, HSI has investigative jurisdiction over all laws governing border control, customs, trade, and immigration and some ICE agents are cross-designated to investigate counternarcotics crimes in coordination with DEA with a clearly articulable nexus to the border. ICE/HSI has a wide range of investigative priorities which combat TCOs engaged in illicit trade, travel, and finance. TCOs employ infinite resources to build their capacity to conduct illicit activity. ICE routinely encounters criminal organizations that deploy sophisticated support structures and invest heavily into ensuring an uninterrupted capacity to smuggle large amounts of people, contraband, and money across our Nation's borders as evidenced by the use of tunnels, aircraft, self-propelled semi-submersibles, corruption, technology, and other capital intensive practices to perpetuate criminal activity. With ICE's authority spanning over 400 Federal statutes, ICE disrupts and dismantles TCOs both domestically and internationally through its Special Agent in Charge (SAC) offices and with its Attaché offices through the investigation of complex TCOs that exploit vulnerabilities at our Nation's land, sea, and air borders. ICE special agents utilize their authority, expertise, and investigative techniques of certified undercover operations, Title III wire intercepts, informants, asset identification and removal, financial and trade information exploitation, and others to not only identify and dismantle TCOs, but deny these organizations their capacity and structure to regenerate the resources and capital needed to survive.

The ICE Northern Border SAC offices and attachés in Canada serve as the base of operations for all of ICE's efforts to identify, disrupt, and dismantle TCOs whose criminal activities have a clearly articulable nexus to the U.S. and Canadian border. The SAC offices that cover the Northern Border include SAC Seattle, SAC Denver, SAC St. Paul, SAC Chicago, SAC Detroit, SAC Buffalo, and SAC Boston.

Air and Marine

Recognizing the vulnerabilities in the air and marine environment along the U.S. and Canadian border, ICE conducts investigations that target TCOs that seek to exploit these vulnerabilities. The following are adjudicated case examples of ICE's successes:

- In June 2008, the Blaine Border Enforcement Security Task Force (BEST) received information concerning multiple suspects involved in narcotics trafficking. Through surveillance, Blaine BEST investigators discovered a beach-front residence located south of Blaine, Washington, bearing evidence of involvement in smuggling via watercraft. The investigation culminated in a five-day surveillance operation in which BEST and Integrated Border Enforcement Team (IBET) investigators seized 111 kilograms of cocaine that were set to be exported to Canada aboard a Sea-Doo watercraft.

Intelligence and Information Sharing

In addition to the important role ICE has at EPIC, SOD, the OCDETF Fusion Center, the IOC-2 and others, ICE utilizes SAC Intelligence Groups located in Boston, Buffalo, Chicago, Denver, Detroit, St. Paul, and Seattle to bolster ICE's efforts to share intelligence and information on the Northern border.

At and Between Ports of Entry

ICE is involved in several key programs that impact at the border and in between the border operations; to include:

Border Enforcement Security Task Force: The first BEST was created by ICE in 2005 as a mechanism to address the threat of cross-border crime along the Southwest border. The BEST are means to combine ICE's broad legal and jurisdictional authorities related to the border with those of other federal, state, county, and local law enforcement agencies to investigate the underlying criminal activities associated with border violence. Since that time, the BEST program has become and remains a proven flexible platform from which ICE, and its task force partners, investigates and targets not only TCOs, but any emerging threat attempting to exploit vulnerabilities at the nation's borders. The BESTs provide a co-located investigative compliment to already existing multi-agency task forces by virtue of their physical proximity to the border. Since its inception, the BEST program has now been expanded to locations on the Northern Border, at our nation's seaports, and to the ICE HSI Attache office in Mexico City. In addition to ICE, the BESTs on the Northern border, currently located in Blaine, Washington; Detroit, Michigan; and Buffalo, New York, include representatives from the following U.S. law enforcement agencies: CBP, U.S. Coast Guard (USCG), Drug Enforcement Administration (DEA), the Bureau of Alcohol, Tobacco, Firearms, and Explosives (ATF), Federal Bureau of Investigation (FBI), the U.S. Postal Inspection Service (USPIS), and the National Oceanic and Atmospheric Administration (NOAA), eight state, local, and county law enforcement agencies are represented. Canadian law enforcement participation includes representatives from the RCMP, (CBSA, Ontario Provincial Police (OPP), Niagara Regional Police Service, Windsor Police Service, Peel Regional Police Service, and the Toronto Police Service. In addition, ICE expects to commence BEST operations in Massena, New York, and at the Seattle Seaport during FY 2011.

The use of these partnerships enables U.S. and Canadian law enforcement agencies to identify threats, address vulnerabilities, and identify, investigate, disrupt, and dismantle transnational criminal organizations in a cohesive and coordinated environment. In addition, through the use of the Title 19 Customs Cross-Designation Program, ICE cross-designates U.S. and Canadian law enforcement officers as "customs officers" to enforce customs laws in the U.S., thereby essentially overcoming the jurisdictional restrictions of the physical border. This cross-designation authority 19 enables foreign, state, and local officers across the country to supplement the ICE investigative mission relating to customs law, to participate on task forces throughout the U.S. and to conduct joint investigations of, among other crimes, narcotics smuggling, and money laundering to disrupt and dismantle criminal organizations threatening this country's borders. There are currently three BESTs operating along the Northern border.

Integrated Border Enforcement Teams: The IBETs operate as intelligence-driven enforcement teams comprised of personnel from ICE, CBP, CBSA, RCMP, and USCG. There are IBET regions along the Northern border. The IBETs actively shares information and works bi-national enforcement operations aimed at securing the U.S.-Canada border. As a core member of the IBET program, ICE is committed to supporting the IBET mission through its investigative offices located along the Northern border.

Tribal Lands

There are three Native American Indian Reservations that have an immediate nexus to the Canadian Border: St. Regis Mohawk Indian Reservation in New York, Blackfeet Indian Reservation in Montana, and the Chippewa Bay Mills Indian Reservation in Michigan. Recognizing that partnerships with Native American Tribes are vital to the investigation of TCOs that utilize Tribal Lands to perpetuate their criminal activity, ICE SAC offices have taken the following steps to ensure the partnerships remain viable and to mitigate the vulnerabilities in these lands:

- The ICE Shadow Wolves are Native American ICE Tactical Officers assigned to the Tohono O'odham Indian Reservation in Arizona who utilize both technology and the ancient art of tracking to investigate drug smugglers. The Shadow Wolves have established relationships with members of the Blackfeet (Montana) and Chippewa Bay Mills (Michigan) reservations.

- ICE worked in FY 2011 to establish its Massena, New York BEST. Once operational, the Massena BEST will serve to unite and coordinate the efforts of key Federal, state, local, tribal, and foreign law enforcement entities to combat the threats and vulnerabilities identified in the SAC Buffalo area of responsibility (AOR). The objective of the Massena BEST is to target, dismantle, and disrupt the most egregious smuggling organizations operating within and along the New York-Ontario border with an emphasis on the area incorporating the Akwesasne Mohawk Indian Reservation, the St. Lawrence River, and the Massena Port of Entry. The Massena BEST anticipates the participation of CBP Office of Field Operations and Office of Border Patrol, New York State Police, USCG, ATF, DEA, RCMP, and CBSA.

- ICE SAC offices that have Tribal Lands in their AORs continue to coordinate with Tribal law enforcement authorities to investigate TOC.

Investigations and Prosecutions

The following is an adjudicated case example of ICE utilizing not only its full investigative capacity to identify, disrupt, and dismantle TCOs, but also working collaboratively with multiple U.S. and Canadian law enforcement and prosecutors to stop pervasive cross-border criminal activity.

- Beginning in 2005, ICE targeted the British Columbia based UN Gang. The UN Gang is a violent, multi-ethnic criminal organization operating from the Lower Mainland of British Columbia, Canada. The UN Gang is involved in narcotics trafficking and money laundering activities throughout the U.S., Canada, Mexico, Venezuela, Colombia, India, Vietnam, Australia, and Great Britain, and was led by Clayton Franklin Roueche. Specifically, the UN Gang imports Canadian-grown marijuana into the U.S. and exports cocaine from the U.S. into Canada. The UN Gang exported hundreds of pounds of cocaine to British Columbia, Canada each month. The UN Gang also facilitates the laundering of illicit proceeds. After Canadian marijuana is smuggled into the U.S., it is sold for U.S. dollars, and these proceeds are provided to couriers who transport the bulk currency to California. The proceeds are used to purchase cocaine, which is then smuggled into Canada and subsequently sold for Canadian dollars. During the course of this investigation, ICE identified several means used by the organization to transport, conceal, and distribute its narcotics. These include the use of privately owned helicopters, fixed-wing airplanes, four wheel drive pickup trucks, and cars outfitted with concealed compartments. According to law enforcement, it is estimated the UN Gang receives up to $2 million Canadian dollars per week in suspected cocaine distribution proceeds at locations in British Columbia, Canada.

- Since December 2005, the ICE investigation of Roueche and other members of the UN Gang resulted in the seizure of 2,169 pounds of marijuana, 335 kilograms of cocaine, 2 pounds of crack cocaine, 4 pounds of meth, 5 firearms, and approximately $2 million.

- On May 17, 2008, U.S., Canadian, and Mexican law enforcement officials worked in close cooperation to arrest Roueche based on a criminal indictment for charges of narcotics trafficking and money laundering. On December 16, 2009, Roueche was sentenced in the U.S. District Court in Seattle, Washington, to 30 years of confinement and five years probation after pleading guilty on April 28, 2009, to exportation of cocaine, importation of marijuana, and conspiracy to launder money.

Department of Homeland Security
U.S. Immigration and Customs Enforcement

Program: Homeland Security Investigations – Intelligence

FY 2011 Enacted funding level ($ 000): $1,096

Program Description:

Key to ICE's efforts to share intelligence and information regarding the Northern border are the SAC Intelligence Groups located in Boston, Buffalo, Chicago, Denver, Detroit, St. Paul, and Seattle. Additional ICE Intelligence programs supporting this endeavor include:

- Integrated National Security Intelligence Teams (INSETs). INSET is an ICE Intelligence program that is designed to increase the capacity for the collection, sharing, and analysis of intelligence among partners with respect to individuals and entities that are a threat to national security; to create an enhanced investigative capacity to bring such individuals and entities to justice; to enhance partner agencies collective ability to combat national security threats; and to meet all specific mandate responsibilities consistent with the laws of Canada and the Charter of Rights and Freedoms.

- Participation in the Strategic Alliance Group Criminal Intelligence Advisory Group (CIAG). Through the CIAG, ICE Intelligence partners with the FBI, DEA, RCMP, UK's Serious Organized Crime Agency, New Zealand Federal Police, Australian Federal Police, and the Australian Crime Commission to produce collaborative threat assessments and exchange any intelligence or targeting information. Additionally, this forum has helped to increase information flow with RCMP on common threats, and helped facilitate the development of a secure communications mechanism, based on the Secret Internet Protocol Router Network, to exchange classified information among CIAG partners.

Department of Homeland Security
U.S. Immigration and Customs Enforcement

Program: Homeland Security Investigations – Office of International Affairs

FY 2011 Enacted funding level ($ 000): $380

Program Description:

Recognizing the vulnerabilities in the air and marine environment along the U.S. and Canadian border, ICE conducts investigations that target TOC organizations that seek to exploit these vulnerabilities.

Intelligence and Information Sharing

The Attaché in Ottawa and the Assistant Attaché offices in Vancouver, Toronto, and Montreal work closely with other Federal entities and their Canadian counterparts, particularly, RCMP, and act as a conduit for ICE and Canadian law enforcement interaction and information sharing.

- On June 20, 1984, the United States and Canada signed a Customs Mutual Assistance Agreement (CMAA) in place between the United States and Canada.). The CMAA allows for the exchange of information, intelligence, and documents that will ultimately assist countries in the prevention and investigation of customs offenses and serves as the primary agreement in place between the two countries.

- On February 19, 2002, he Statement of Mutual Understanding on Information Sharing between Department of State, Immigration and Naturalization Service, and Department of Citizenship and Immigration Canada was signed. This is an agreement which allows for the sharing of personal information to assist in the effective administration and enforcement of the Participants' citizenship and immigration laws; to facilitate the secure flow of people to Canada or the United States through co-operative border management among the Participants; to promote international justice and security by fostering respect for human rights and by denying access to the United States and Canada to persons who are criminals or security risks for the enforcement of Immigration laws.

- On November 10, 2010, ICE Director Morton, Deputy CBP Commissioner Aguilar, and then-CBSA President Rigby signed the ICE/CBP/CBSA Currency Seizure Information Sharing Memorandum of Understanding (MOU). This MOU allows for the sharing of currency seizure information on a case by case basis in real time.

Department of Homeland Security
U.S. Coast Guard

Program: USCG – Drug Interdiction

FY 2011 Enacted funding level ($ 000): $12,507[11]

Program Description:

The U.S. Coast Guard's (USCG) efforts support the National Drug Control Strategy across all regions, including the Southwest border, transit zone, and Northern border. The USCG's overall strategy is to employ a layered approach to maritime security by forward deploying cutters and aircraft close to the source zone of the contraband and near our maritime borders in the U.S. USCG's drug interdiction objective is to reduce the flow of illegal drugs entering the U.S. through the Northern and Southern borders by denying smugglers access to maritime routes. Additionally, the USCG leverages U.S. Navy and Allied nation ships to enhance presence and to expand interdiction opportunities by embarking law enforcement detachments on these platforms. These operations are conducted deep in the Caribbean and Eastern Pacific closer to the source zone along the major trafficking maritime routes from South and Central America, Mexico, and the Antilles. Working with the Department of Defense's U.S. Southern Command via the Joint Interagency Task Force- South (JIATF-S), the USCG deploys assets to interdict the maritime conveyances prior to them reaching their transshipment destinations in Central America, Mexico, and geographic areas located further north. FY 2011 resources support the operation and maintenance of existing cutters, aircraft, boats, Command, Control, Communications, Computers, Intelligence, Surveillance, and Reconnaissance (C4ISR) systems, infrastructure, and people for execution of the illegal drug interdiction mission. FY 2011 resources also support the recapitalization of aged, obsolete, and unreliable assets. Continued investment in recapitalization is the Coast Guard's top budget priority.

The USCG has several long term initiatives intended to enhance drug interdiction effectiveness along the Northern border. Of note, the Integrated Cross-border Maritime Law Enforcement Framework Agreement (ICMLEO ShipRider) was signed by both DHS and the Canadian Border Security Agency (CBSA) in May 2009. The ICMLEO ShipRider is the maritime operational arm of the IBET. As the principal U.S. agency and designated Central Authority for this agreement, the USCG has developed international training and participated in several successful exercises since 2005, most recently conducting maritime security operations during the June 2010 G20 Summit in Toronto, Ontario. When ratified by the Canadian government, the program will facilitate cross-designation of law enforcement authorities for trained officers from each participating nation, creating fully integrated law enforcement teams. This concept virtually minimizes impediments to cross-border law enforcement for both nations. Additionally, the program acts as a force multiplier by removing patrolling redundancies along each side of the border.

---

11. As the USCG does not apportion its Drug Control Budget by region, the Northern border funding amount shown is an estimate based on USCG operations impacting the flow of illegal drugs across the Northern border. By examining the USCG level of effort in applicable areas, the USCG estimates that 1% of resources are devoted to the Northern border.

The agreement allows for future expansion of these authorities to other Federal, state, local, and tribal partners.

The USCG participates in numerous joint counterdrug operations along the Northern border that are focused on preventing illegal contraband from being smuggled to the U.S. and Canada. In the Great Lakes, the USCG conducts joint operations with Federal, state, local and tribal law enforcement during surge operations such as Channel Watch, Northern Shore, Northern Border Initiative, and Vigilant Enforcer. Each of these operations are coordinated with the RCMP and designed to provide a robust law enforcement presence along the shared border with Canada by targeting maritime smuggling in a specific area. In the Northwest maritime region, the USCG is developing a strategy and long standing operation, which will target cross border maritime smuggling through the Straits of Juan de Fuca and Strait of Georgia with participation from Federal, state and local law enforcement authorities and RCMP.

Department of Justice
Criminal Division

Program: Criminal Division

FY 2011 Enacted funding level ($ 000): $2,554

Program Description:

The Criminal Division develops, enforces, and supervises the application of all Federal criminal laws, except those specifically assigned to other divisions. The Division and the 93 U.S. Attorneys are responsible for overseeing criminal matters under more than 900 statutes, as well as certain civil litigation. The Criminal Division supports the President's *National Drug Control Strategy* as well as the *National Northern Border Counternarcotics Strategy*. Below are examples how the Division supports these efforts:

- The Division's Narcotic and Dangerous Drug Section (NDDS) works closely with the DEA Attaché for the Ottawa Country Office and with Canadian law enforcement officials and prosecutors in investigating and prosecuting cross-border drug trafficking offenses against the U.S. Canada is a significant producer of marijuana and supplier of Ecstasy for domestic use and export to the U.S. In particular, the rise of meth production in Canada is a concern for the U.S. and an area that requires continued bilateral cooperation.

- During FY 2011, NDDS indicted a Canadian-based drug trafficking organization for conspiracy to import Ecstasy and marijuana into the U.S. in violation of 21 U.S.C. § 952, 959, 960, and 963. A second indictment currently is pending in an Organized Crime Drug Enforcement Task Force-designated case also charging a conspiracy to import Ecstasy and marijuana into the U.S. In addition, there are forfeiture allegations contained in the indictments. A third case continues in the investigative stage. These bilateral investigations involve U.S. law enforcement agencies including ICE, DEA, FBI, CBP, and the USCG, as well as members of the OPP, the RCMP, and various other Canadian law enforcement agencies.

- NDDS will continue to collaborate with Canadian authorities to investigate and prosecute international drug trafficking organizations operating along the Northern border. Furthermore, the Special Operations Division (SOD) supports all multi-district, multi-national investigations targeting narcotics trafficking along the Northern border.

- The Office of International Affairs (OIA) serves as the United States' central authority for all formal requests for mutual legal assistance and through extradition, or other lawful methods, secures the return of fugitives to the United States from abroad and returns fugitives from foreign justice to the countries from which they fled. Because of our close proximity, has led there is a heavy volume of extradition and MLAT requests, at the Federal, state, and local level. Indeed, there is a robust and sophisticated practice in extraditions and MLATs between the U.S. and Canada, historically one of our busiest treaty partners. Flight across the border to avoid prosecution is a regular occurrence. In 2010, with regard to extradition and legal assistance, about half of the extradition requests sent to Canada, and about a quarter of MLAT requests to Canada, involved narcotics offenses.

- In FY 2010, 71 fugitives were returned from Canada of whom 31 were wanted for narcotics offenses. With 69 fugitives returned as of July 2011, of whom 25 were wanted for narcotics offenses, the Division is on track to meet or exceed FY 2010 accomplishments in FY 2011.

- OIA works on a wide range of law enforcement matters affecting the U.S. and Canada, such as drug trafficking (movement of marijuana and ecstasy from Canada to the U.S. and cocaine and firearms from the U.S. into Canada); counterterrorism; and significant white collar crime cases, including telemarketing fraud (lottery scams and securities fraud) originating in Canada and targeting the elderly in the U.S.

- The Attorney General, the Secretary for Homeland Security, the Canadian Minister of Public Safety, and the Canadian Minister of Justice meet annually for the CBCF Ministerial, most recently in November 2010. Smaller working-level meetings take place throughout the year and bring together more than 100 senior law enforcement officials and prosecutors from Canada and the U.S. to address cross-border issues, including counterterrorism cooperation, mass-marketing fraud, interoperability of our respective law enforcement agencies along the border, and combating organized crime (such as drug trafficking). At the November 2010 CBCF Ministerial, the Ministers initiated a discussion about improving mutual understanding and communication in cross-border undercover operations, and approved the exploration of enhanced cross-border investigations. Meetings on both of these subjects have continued into 2011 (January and June), and the discussions with Canada concerning undercover operations have been especially productive thus far. The next CBCF Ministerial is scheduled tentatively for the Fall of 2011 in Ottawa, Ontario.

- In February 2011, President Obama and Prime Minister Harper signed issued a declaration entitled *Beyond the Border: A Shared Vision for Perimeter Security and Economic Competitiveness* to pursue a joint perimeter approach to security, work together at and away from the borders to enhance security, and accelerate the legitimate flow of people, goods, and services between the two countries. The National Security Staff (NSS), in coordination with DOJ/OIA, DHS, and other agencies, has led the development of a 32-point "action plan," and its 32 separate templates for each initiative agreed to by the President and Prime Minister. DOJ has been involved in some of these action plans being discussed as part of this initiative, including issues concerning intelligence/information sharing, NextGen, radio interoperability, and privacy.

- The Division's Organized Crime and Gang Section (OCGS) regularly investigates domestic and international organized crime entities that have Northern border implications. In FY 2011, for instance, OCGS attorneys handled a Florida-based investigation and prosecution where a defendant has provided information about a Canadian drug supplier. Similarly, an OCGS investigation into a traditional La Cosa Nostra (LCN) organized crime entity has developed information that the LCN members use a Canadian source-of-supply for marijuana trafficking. A Vietnamese organization operating in and around Philadelphia was also prosecuted by OCGS, with several targets in Canada indicted and subject to extradition proceedings.

Department of Justice
Drug Enforcement Administration

Program: Drug Enforcement Administration

FY 2011 Enacted funding level ($ 000): $164,806

Program Description:

The Drug Enforcement Administration (DEA) dedicates $164.8 million of its resources and approximately 436 of its special agents to the Northern border, as well as hundreds of task force officers assigned to DEA Northern border office enforcement groups.

Drug Trafficking is the single largest source of criminal proceeds generated by U.S./Canada cross-border activity. The Divisions that support the Northern border are Seattle Division, Denver Division, Chicago Division, Detroit Division, Philadelphia Division, New York Division, and the Boston Division. These DEA offices continue to utilize co-located task forces as a force multiplier to investigate CPOT level organizations that operate along the Northern border. Furthermore, DEA is the single point of contact for U.S. drug related matters in the foreign environment and for ensuring that investigations comply with relevant U.S. and Canadian government protocols.

The DEA will continue to focus Federal resources on the disruption or dismantlement of drug trafficking organizations that control the illegal drug trade and the seizure of the proceeds and assets involved in the illegal drug trade along the Northern border. DEA-led Special Operations Division (SOD) will continue to coordinate the major investigations conducted along the Northern border in concert with the DEA Attaché in Ottawa.

Established in 1994, SOD is a DEA-led, multi-agency, operations coordination center with participation from Federal law enforcement agencies, the Department of Defense, the Intelligence Community, and international law enforcement partners. SOD's mission is to establish strategies and operations to dismantle national and international trafficking organizations by attacking their command and control communications. Special emphasis is placed on those major drug trafficking and narco-terrorism organizations that operate across jurisdictional boundaries on a regional, national, and international level. SOD provides foreign- and domestic-based law enforcement agents with timely investigative information that enables them to fully exploit Federal law enforcement's investigative authority under Title III of the U.S. Code. SOD coordinates overlapping investigations, ensuring that tactical and operational intelligence is deconflicted and shared between law enforcement agencies.

Additionally, in FY2010, DOJ's National Gang Targeting, Enforcement, and Coordination Center (GangTECC) was partnered with the Special Operations Division. Under the operational umbrella of SOD, the new gang section has quickly been incorporated into SOD's attack strategy focused on gangs and has been coordinating investigations on such organizations as the Hells Angels and other motorcycle gangs that are operating along the Northern border. Under Operation Fallen Angels, an SOD/GangTECC investigation targeting the Hells Angels motorcycles gang, results to date for this ongoing investigation include 20 arrests, and seizures of over $3.5M in currency, 108 kilos of cocaine, 2,554 pounds of marijuana, four aircrafts, and 26 weapons.

In May 2011, SOD coordinated a takedown of Operation Xpressway, a multi-jurisdictional, multi-agency Organized Crime Drug Enforcement Task Force (OCDETF) operation targeting the Trang Looc Organization, a Vietnamese TCO responsible for the importation of Ecstasy from Canada and meth from Mexico for distribution within California and Hawaii, and transported cocaine and meth to Vancouver, Canada, in exchange for Ecstasy and bulk currency. Operation Xpressway resulted in 66 arrests and the seizure of 83 kilograms of cocaine, 18 pounds of meth, 857,000 Ecstasy tablets, 75 kilograms of MDMA powder, 1,370 marijuana plants, 110 pounds of marijuana, $1.8 million in bulk currency, $1.2 million in assets, 3 vehicles, and 23 weapons. The success of this multi-jurisdictional, multi-agency wire intercept investigation depended on timely cooperation between domestic and foreign law enforcement entities throughout Canada, Mexico, and United States.

SOD is also coordinating Operation Tomahawk, targeting traffickers operating in and around Native American reservations. As part of this operation, DEA, with the assistance of the Internal Revenue Service, has been investigating a large scale marijuana trafficking organization that is believed to be responsible for the importation of 300-500 pounds of marijuana from Canada on a monthly basis. During the course of the investigation, agents and task force officers recovered over 270 pounds of marijuana, 29 firearms, approximately $290,000 cash and 21 vehicles or other conveyances. As a result of this investigation the United States Attorney's Office for Northern District of New York indicted 16 individuals on charges of Possession with intent to Distribute Marijuana and Conspiracy to Possess and Distribute Marijuana. On May 3, 2011, agents and officers executed the arrest warrants without incident.

The DEA's mission is to enforce the controlled substance laws and regulations of the U.S. and bring to the criminal and civil justice system of the U.S., or any other competent jurisdiction, those organizations and principal members of organizations involved in the growing, manufacturing, or distribution of controlled substances appearing in or destined for illicit traffic in the U.S., including organizations that use drug trafficking proceeds to finance terror; and to recommend and support programs aimed at reducing the availability of and demand for illicit controlled substances on the domestic and international markets.

Furthermore, as part of a Country Team within the United States Embassy, the DEA Country Attaché acts as the focal point with Canadian law enforcement officials on drug law enforcement intelligence and investigative matters. This role assures coordination, maximizes investigative effectiveness, promotes agents' safety, and unifies the United States Government's drug control efforts undertaken in Canada. To that end, DEA is responsible for ensuring: (a) that the foreign extensions of all United States drug investigations are coordinated properly within the United States Embassy in Canada, as well as with the relevant host country law enforcement authorities; and, (b) that the foreign extension of any federal drug investigation complies with all relevant protocols of the United States Government and Canada.

DEA's Information and Intelligence Sharing Capabilities:

The El Paso Intelligence Center (EPIC) has a robust program to provide responses to questions about illicit activity in the United States. EPIC has provided responses to 141 Requests for Information to U.S. Law Enforcement along the Northern Border during the past 18 months. There were also four requests, three from the Royal Canadian Mounted Police and one from the DEA Vancouver office.

The Domestic Highway Enforcement Unit (DHE) at the El Paso Intelligence Center supports the northern border by developing actionable intelligence products i.e. DEA cable, TECs Alert, Tactical Incident Notification (TIN), and LPR Alerts for federal, state, and local Law Enforcement through analytical targeting of seizure events reported to the National Seizure System.

The DEA National LPR program is a complex camera and alerting system that is used as an investigative tool to monitor and target roadway conveyances commonly used to transport bulk cash and other contraband. The LPR system provides images and data in real-time as vehicles transit a strategically placed License Plate Reader point. The program promotes information sharing and coordination through a de-confliction mechanism, which notifies the appropriate parties when common links are identified across multiple investigations. The LPR initiative is available to all Federal, state, and local law enforcement officers through EPIC.

The EPIC Air Investigative Unit supports Northern Border LE operations. The unit currently has Mode S aircraft tracking devices in support of the Spokane, WA and Holton, ME areas. Additionally, The Air Investigative Unit has requests for Mode S installs in support of Havre, MT and Detroit. The unit also provided CBP, Holton, ME with a spread sheet of aircraft transiting the area for their review. The CBP will use this to establish tracking priorities for suspect aircraft in the area.

The EPIC Research and Analysis Section is working with the DEA Ottawa Country Office, and Canadian LE, to the concept of the Gatekeeper initiative and the feasibility of using this as a base for a Northern Border Model. This section also provides support to DEA Ottawa, and DEA Northern border, for example the DEA Seattle Division, on cases which have links from the Northern border to Mexico.

Department of Justice
National Drug Intelligence Center

Program: Northern Border

FY 2011 Enacted funding level ($ 000): $109

Program Description:

During FY 2011 (October –June), the National Drug Intelligence Center (NDIC) has had up to two intelligence analysts devoting approximately 40 – 90 percent of their time to Northern border issues. Work performed includes drafting a Northern Border Assessment for the Organized Crime Drug Enforcement Task Force and participating in ONDCP's Northern Border Strategy Working Group. Within ONDCP's working group, NDIC has been working with the Drug Enforcement Administration in preparing a threat assessment that will be included in the strategy.

NDIC's mission is to provide strategic domestic drug-related intelligence support to the drug control, public health, law enforcement, and intelligence communities of the U.S. NDIC provides domestic and strategic counterdrug analysis by information from materials gathered in Federal, state, and local law enforcement activities associated with counterdrug, counterterrorism, and national security investigations and operations.

Department of Justice
Interagency Crime Drug Enforcement

Program: Organized Crime Drug Enforcement Task Force (OCDETF)

FY 2011 Enacted funding level ($ 000): $59,793

Program Description:

All of the Organized Crime Drug Enforcement Task Force's (OCDETF) Northern border-related cases are conducted by prosecutor-led multi-agency task forces. OCDETF uses its resources to support the investigative activities of the following participating agencies: Bureau of Alcohol, Tobacco, Firearms, and Explosives; Drug Enforcement Administration; Federal Bureau of Investigation; and the U.S. Marshals Service. These figures do not include OCDETF resources committed to the Northern border by the Department of Homeland Security or the Internal Revenue Service (IRS), which receive their OCDETF funding in their individual appropriations and are not administered by the OCDETF Executive Office. It also utilizes its reimbursable prosecutorial resources situated at the 94 U.S. Attorneys' offices around the country, which are executed through the Executive Office for U.S. Attorneys (EOUSA), and at the Criminal Division of the Department of Justice, which is executed through attorneys in the Criminal Division and the OCDETF Executive Office) for Northern border prosecutorial activities. Approximately 16 percent of OCDETF investigations are Northern border-related. At the beginning of FY 2010, OCDETF implemented a new policy that requires a financial investigation to have been started prior to the approval and receipt of an OCDETF designation. Therefore, one hundred percent of OCDETF investigations initiated in FY 2010 have an active financial component. As a result of OCDETF investigations, nearly $41 million was seized in the states bordering Canada in FY 2010.

Intelligence and Information Sharing

The OCDETF Program promotes intelligence sharing and intelligence-driven enforcement and strives to achieve maximum impact through strategic planning and operational coordination. OCDETF has long recognized that no single law enforcement entity is in a position to disrupt and dismantle sophisticated drug and money laundering organizations alone. OCDETF combines the resources and expertise of its seven Federal agency members—ATF, DEA, FBI, USMS, IRS, ICE, and the USCG—in cooperation with the Department of Justice's Criminal Division, the 94 U.S. Attorneys' Offices, and state and local law enforcement, to identify, disrupt, and dismantle the drug trafficking and money laundering organizations most responsible for the Nation's supply of illegal drugs and the violence the drug trade generates and fuels. OCDETF works because it effectively leverages the investigative and prosecutorial strengths of each participant to combat drug-related organized crime. In addition, the OCDETF Fusion Center (OFC) is the cornerstone of OCDETF's intelligence efforts, is funded through the Interagency Crime and Drug Enforcement account and is overseen by the OCDETF Director. The OFC is a comprehensive data center containing all drug and related financial intelligence information from all seven OCDETF-member investigative agencies, and the Financial Crimes Enforcement Network, as well as relevant data from many other agencies. The OFC is designed to conduct cross-agency integration and analysis of the data, to create comprehensive intelligence pictures of targeted organizations, including those identified as Consolidated Priority Organization Targets (CPOTs) and Regional Priority Organization Targets (RPOTs), and to pass actionable leads through the multi-agency Special Operations Division (SOD) to OCDETF participants in the field including the OCDETF Co-located Strike Forces.

Department of Justice
Office of The Federal Detention Trustee

Program: Northern Border

FY 2011 Enacted funding level ($ 000): $42,225

Program Description:

The Office of the Federal Detention Trustee (OFDT) provides funding to the USMS to support housing for persons arrested along the Northern border and detained while awaiting trial. For FY 2011, Northern border drug-related resources were $42.2 million and with an average daily population (ADP) of 1,397. These funding totals are based on population data.

Department of Justice
Office of Justice Programs

Program: Northern Border Prosecutors Initiative

FY 2011 Enacted funding level ($ 000): $2,485

Program Description:

The Northern Border Prosecutors Initiative provides payment to states and local jurisdictions for costs associated with the approved prosecution and pre-trial detention services for cases formally referred to local prosecutors by the U.S. Attorneys' Offices and cases diverted from Federal prosecution. Eligible jurisdictions include the county governments and the fourteen state governments in Alaska, Idaho, Maine, Michigan, Minnesota, Montana, New Hampshire, New York, North Dakota, Ohio, Pennsylvania, Vermont, Washington, and Wisconsin.

Department of Justice
Executive Office For U.S. Attorneys

Program: Prosecutions

FY 2011 Enacted funding level ($ 000): $9,792

Program Description:

The Executive Office for U.S. Attorneys (EOUSA) does not have a specific appropriation for drug control activities. EOUSA's estimated drug expenditures are calculated using attorney and non-attorney full time equivalent (FTE) resources dedicated to non-OCDETF drug prosecutions. This FTE data is captured at the end of the fiscal year using the EOUSA work year tracking and reporting system. For this report, actual work years expended in FY 2010 on non-OCEDETF drug prosecutions along the Northern border are multiplied by EOUSA's cost module to arrive at an estimated base funding level for FY 2011. Estimated expenditures do not include facility costs such as rent and security and do not include overhead costs. EOUSA projects that the same level of FTE will occur in FY 2011 that was used in FY 2010.

The EOUSA offices work in conjunction with law enforcement to disrupt domestic and international drug trafficking and narcotics production through comprehensive investigations and prosecutions of criminal organizations. A core mission of each of the EOUSA office is to prosecute violations of Federal drug trafficking, controlled substance, money laundering, and related Federal laws in order to deter continued illicit drug distribution and use in the U.S. This mission includes utilization of the grand jury process to investigate and to uncover the criminal conduct at issue and the subsequent presentation of the evidence in court as part of prosecution of individuals and organizations who violate Federal law. The EOUSA offices will continue to work with law enforcement within available funding levels and support the prosecution of violators of drug-related activities.

Department of Justice
U.S. Marshals Service

Program: Northern Border

FY 2011 Enacted funding level ($ 000): $23,724

Program Description:

The U.S. Marshals Service (USMS) occupies a uniquely central position in the Federal justice system. It is the enforcement arm of the Federal courts, and as such, it is involved in virtually every Federal law enforcement initiative. Therefore, the USMS plays a role in supporting the *National Northern Border Counternarcotics Strategy*. In conjunction with its relevant core functions in executing drug warrants, transporting and securing prisoners, and protecting the judiciary, the USMS operates the Canadian Investigative Liaison program to facilitate fugitive apprehensions along the Northern border and throughout all of Canada.

The purpose of the Canada Investigative Liaison program is to facilitate transnational fugitive investigations between the U.S. and Canada. The USMS provides Deputy U.S. Marshals, who have been trained in Canadian legal procedures and protocols, to work with Canadian law enforcement agencies toward apprehension of these wanted individuals. The USMS facilitates fugitive investigations with Canada through a Senior Inspector at USMS Headquarters within the Investigative Operations Division, International Investigations Branch, as well as sixteen (16) Canada Investigative Liaison investigators, located in each Federal judicial district across the Northern border and Alaska. Since 2003, the USMS has extradited or deported nearly 800 fugitives of which approximately 40 percent have had a nexus to illegal narcotics-related offenses. Presently, the USMS has an active caseload of approximately 225 investigations in Canada of which approximately 40 percent have a nexus to illegal narcotics related offenses.

Funding Detail:

The USMS does not have a specific appropriation for drug interaction activities; however, the Salaries and Expenses (S&E) appropriation is internally allocated to: 1) judicial and courthouse security to carry out the USMS judicial security mission; 2) task forces to carry out the USMS fugitive apprehension mission; and 3) to district offices to carry out the USMS prisoner security and transportation mission. USMS resource estimates for drug control are based on the agency's drug-related workload. For Judicial and Courthouse Security as well as Prisoner Security and Transportation, 18 percent of in-custody prisoners have a drug-related charge, of which the Northern border comprises 8 percent. For Fugitive Apprehension, 31 percent of warrants cleared are drug-related, of which the Northern border comprises 10 percent. These percentages are applied to S&E appropriation to formulate drug-related resources. S&E resources include employee payroll, rent, and operating expenses. The FY 2011 enacted budget inclusive of the rescission is $1.1 billion, the drug related portion is $254.7 million, and the Northern border portion is $23.7 million.

Department of Transportation
Federal Aviation Administration

Program: Air Traffic Organization/ En Route and Oceanic Services

FY 2011 Enacted funding level ($ 000): $456

Program Description:

The Air Traffic Organization (ATO), in support of the *National Northern Border Counternarcotics Strategy*, is to monitor the Air Defense Identification Zone (ADIZ). The ADIZ is the area of airspace defined by the U.S. within which the ready identification, location, and control of aircraft is required in the interest of national security. Typically, an aircraft entering the ADIZ is required to radio its planned course, destination, and any additional details about its trip through the ADIZ to authorities.

Air traffic controllers that staff the Air Route Traffic Control Centers (ARTCCs) monitor the ADIZ to detect possible suspicious aircraft movement. When suspicious movement is identified, ARTCC staff notifies the DEA and the USCG of such activity. When FAA receives confirmation of suspicious aircraft movement from the DEA/USCG, controllers support interdiction efforts by providing radar vectors to track time of arrival, traffic advisory information, and last known positions to intercept the aircraft of interest.

ARTCC staff supports DEA and USCG in preplanned interdiction efforts through the establishment of temporary flight restriction areas, which is often on a real-time basis. ATO also supports DEA and USCG during training exercises.

Cost estimates are solely attributed to personnel costs for air traffic controllers at ARTCC facilities.